# From MySpace™ to My Place:

## The Ladies' Guide to Finding Mr. Right or Mr. Right Now Online

Written by Flyness

**YOUR ALL OUT GUIDE
FOR MEETING THAT QUALITY GUY ONLINE!**

# THANKS:

*I would like to thank all of my friends, family, 'The Princess', Miss Fray and send a special thanks to all of the lovely ladies I met online who've kept my game "crisp," along with my "true-to-the-game" macks who help me stay on my game. Keep it P-I.*

There was a lot of time and effort that went into putting this book together. The process of putting the material together took many hours over the course of many weeks. That means that this information has value, and your friends, neighbors, and co-workers may want to share it. The price of this book is very small, compared to the value you are getting from it. So if your friends like the concept of the book, please encourage them to purchase their own copy from www.MyspaceToMyPlace.com.

From MySpace to My Place: The Ladies' Guide to Finding Mr. Right or Mr. Right Now Online, by Flyness
Flyness Publishing

ISBN: 978-0-578-01938-3

# Table of Contents

# Introduction

At the end of 2007, I wrote and published, *From MySpace to My Place: The Men's Guide to Snagging Women Online.* In the introduction of that book, I talked about my childhood as a kid who attended five schools in six years with a lack of social prowess. From a very young age, I began dialing local chatlines and going on blind dates with women I had just met. Gradually, I moved to AOL chatrooms in the mid 90's and eventually to about every social networking site known to man.

*From MySpace to My Place: The Men's Guide to Snagging Women Online* was easily written due to the vast experiences I had during hundreds of online to in-person meetings with women. In fact, I highly recommend that book to both my male *and* female readers alike (you may get both of these books by going to www.myspacetomyplace.com or by visiting your local bookstore). Though geared toward men, that book is a favorite among women as well, as it offers an inside glimpse into the mind of a man and things he must stay cognizant of in the dating arena. Plus with the increasing numbers of men getting this book, it might be wise to learn what he's reading. ;)

Unlike that book, *The Ladies' Guide to Finding Mr. Right or Mr. Right Now Online* has involved quite a bit of research. After releasing my previous book, I immediately began surveying women on their thoughts on online dating—specifically when it came to social networking sites, such as MySpace, Facebook, Friendster and the like. Online dating, specifically through social networking sites, is something that has been *rarely* discussed in the public light. However, as I began meeting dozens of women off the internet, writing these books was just something that made sense.

Though I consider myself a *jedi* in the online dating world, getting into a woman's brain on this subject was both challenging and enlightening. The infusion of my own experiences along with my various conversations with women gave birth to this book.

Lastly, I always add a twist and a bit of flare. Ladies, I love each and every one of you (really, I do). But unlike too many other relationship books, I will _not_ BS you. There will be very little sugarcoating. I am not here to propel you into a fantasy world. I am going to keep it real and I may hurt some feelings. But this book is my best effort to make sure that each and every one of you is on top your game. So curl up on your sofa or bed, shut the door, and proceed with caution. In the meantime, if you have any questions or would like to sign up for one-on-one coaching from me, log on to www.myspacetomyplace.com.

# Chapter One - Your Profile

W elcome to your favorite social networking site—whether that site is MySpace, Friendster, Facebook, Plentyoffish, Localhookupz, Blackplanet, Migente, Asianave, Hi5, or the dozens of others that are out there. I'm sure many, if not most of you have an online page from one of these sites. (If you *don't*, I find it a little strange in this day and age). In any event, it really doesn't matter which site you belong to. Many of you will make dramatic changes to your pages, once you read this book. So first things first; let's start with the question, "What should my page look like?"

### Who Are You?

Before we talk about finding *Mr. Right* or *Mr. Right Now*, it is essential that you get your profile page in order. Else your prospects for encountering quality men will be grim.

There is no ideal profile out there—your page should be the best reflection of you, hands down. While you should never lie or "embellish" any part of your page, you should always aim to bring forth a positive image of yourself at all times. In one of his comedy shows, Chris Rock said that seeing a person for the first time is really seeing their representative. They are emphasizing their strong points. Ladies, the goal of your profile is proper representation. Are you a dancer? Do you like to knit? Do you play ball? Find something you are good at and do not be afraid to display that talent. (This is also a way you can tell if a guy is actually paying attention to *you*).

Whatever the case, you should never try to be something you're not. MySpace (especially) is loaded to the brim with women who claim to be models. Just because you have a MySpace page and 1,000 commenting friends does not make you an internet model. On that subject, statistics show that very few of you are making over $250,000 per year. Get the nonsense off your page.

Here are the top five lies women perpetuate through their profiles:

1. "I'm an Internet Model"
2. Faking physical fitness/Hiding unflattering physical features
3. Age
4. Relationship Status
5. Promiscuity Level

### *"I'm an Internet Model"*

Are you *really* a model? Pertaining to women on social networking sites, there is no bigger lie than the "I'm a model" routine. Taking a bunch of photos at the beach or riverfront does not make you a model. A set of photos taken from Glamour Shots® does not make you a model. This phenomenon is similar to men who claim to be rappers or rock stars the minute they post a demo track online that no ones ever heard of.

The worst part about the majority of self-proclaimed models is the photo quality of their photos. If you are seriously aspiring to be a model, invest in a high-quality photo shoot. Believe it or not there are model scouts who occasionally "peruse" these sites looking for talent. In fact, all of the promo models I used for my last book came from MySpace. One of the young ladies was selected to be in a major hip hop video; yet none of that would have happened if she didn't have her act together. Unless you are getting paid a living wage to model or have serious aspirations, please let this go. If you have serious aspirations to have a career in modeling, throw in the word, "aspiring."

# Faking physical fitness/Hiding unflattering physical features

## *"More to Love" Women*

This is a topic I broke down in Chapter 2 of *The Men's Guide.* In that chapter, I warned men about the deceptive techniques women use online. One of the "biggest" hustles is the way overweight women intentionally deceive men with photos that misrepresent their true size. It is one thing to only take head shots or to have no photo altogether. Technically there's nothing wrong with *omission,* though it is strongly advised to have at least three photos. However, when you are actually doctoring up your look to appear thinner, that is *deception.*

Here are some of the more common deceptive "thinning" techniques you should never resort to:

*Puckering your lips

*Editing the photo to make everything appear thinner

*Using a photo editing program to get rid of body fat

*Using a photo from "back in the day" when you were thinner

*Using someone else's photos

If you are a larger woman, there is no reason to deceive men. While deception may land you more men online, you are setting yourself up for disaster should you two ever meet in person. So in the end, what are you getting out of it? Despite what you look like, you should never try to be (or appear to be) someone who you are not. As I acknowledged in my first book, there are men who do not mind a bigger girl. If you are truly satisfied with your weight, then there's no reason to hide it. If not, take active steps to rectify it and use your profile as a motivator, by posting new pictures as you begin to lose weight. Whatever the case, always be true to yourself.

### Hiding Unflattering Features

Similar to "more to love" women who misrepresent their size, there are plenty of ladies who take it to the extreme and totally alter their appearance for a photo.

A few years before writing this book (before my game was "ultra-crisp"), I met a woman online and used to communicate with her via the webcam. Let's call her Jasmine. After a week or two of chatting online, we decided to go on a double date where she would set her friend up with my friend. Let's call her friend, Jennifer. My friend was very hesitant to meet this girl without at least seeing her photo. After pressing the issue, Jasmine sent us two photos of Jennifer, both of which seemed nice. She appeared to be a size 8 or so, had a cute shape, hair to her shoulders, a cute face and a decent style, all-around.

Yet when my friend and I met these women in person, we were horrified. While Jasmine was extremely attractive as expected, Jennifer looked sort of like "Shrek". For one, she was more than double the size she was in her photos. She also had almost no hair (and the little she had was messy). Her face was a little ragged and her clothes didn't look right. Nevertheless, we went out anyway and though I had a good time with Jasmine, my friend couldn't wait to end the date.

Now ladies, let me say again that there are men out there who will date you regardless of your appearance. However, it's time to acknowledge the reality and "be what you want." This means that you should *upgrade* yourself to the type of man you desire. Please proceed.

### Upgrading

Earlier I mentioned staying true to yourself, despite your outward appearance. Yet in order to have a better selection of the quality men both off and online, you should be actively *upgrading* yourself at every possible moment. To begin, you must first evaluate yourself from the inside out. If you desire a man of means (regardless of being *Mr. Right* or *Mr. Right Now*), you must also bring something to the table as well.

Here are some common questions real men of means conjure up, when they are looking at your profile:

PHYSICAL (essential if you are looking for a quality
*Mr. Right Now*)

*Is she in shape?

*Does she appear to have good hygiene? (skin, hair, and nails)

*Does she have a tight ass?

*Are her breasts perky?

*Is she smiling? Does she appear friendly?

*Does she exude a good degree of sexual energy?

If you can honestly take a look at yourself and answer yes to the majority of these questions, you stand a better shot of *landing* Mr. *Right Now*. If not, it's time to hit the gym and go on a diet.

NON-PHYSICAL (a necessity if you are looking for
a quality *Mr. Right*)

*Is she college educated?

*Does she have her own apartment or home?

*Can she cook?/Is she talented?

*Is she without children?

*Is she career driven?

*Is she fun to be around, nonjudgmental, courteous, and baggage-free?

If you can answer yes to most of these questions, you stand a better shot in *keeping Mr. Right.*

I hate to "throw someone under the bus," or use someone negatively in an example, but the qualities needed to attract and keep a *Mr. Right* are not with Keyshia Cole's family—namely her mother and sister. On her reality show, "The Way It Is" with Keyshia Cole on BET, we get an inside glimpse into her family and her daily struggles. While Keyshia is somewhat attractive and continuously advances her career, her mother and sister are constantly burdened with bad luck.

In addition to the mother's former drug habit and behavioral problems, along with her sister's weight problems, both women are loud, argumentative, baggage-laden and stressed out. Quite honestly speaking, what man of means wants to deal with that? As I will explain more in Chapter 2, there are many men who will *bang you* (have sex with you) without any desire to be with you long term. If you've watched this show, most of the men in these womens' lives do not desire them beyond any short term gratification. Ladies, it is your job to be the lady that *all* men want.

## BAGGAGE HANDLING

Kids happen. Divorce happens. Age happens. There are certain things that happen, many of which we have little or no control over—especially after it has already taken place.

### Weight

It is no secret that weight is a major issue. As I mentioned earlier, faking physical fitness is unacceptable and must be avoided at all costs. Yet if you are overweight, it is necessary to get your weight in order to have the greatest success in landing a quality man.

It is rare that you will ever encounter a man of financial means who settle down and marry a big girl.[1] The answer is simple: because he does not have to. A man with money has substantially more options in the dating field, similar to attractive women. How can you begin to "wow" a man with your intellect and personality if he is not attracted to you in the first place?

Weight is often a reflection of your self image. Too many women turn to food for comfort in the face of stress and anxiety. So ask yourself why would a *Mr. Right* want to be with a woman who cannot be disciplined enough to take care of herself? As hard as it is, you must be vigilant in conquering your weight.

### Children

If you are a mother, having a child something to be proud of. Don't ever *regret* your children.

At the same time, you should be careful about the choices you make and the responsibilities you must uphold as a lady. Modern day television is loaded with talk shows featuring women who are blaming all of the "no good men" out there for not being responsible fathers. While a valid argument, I find myself becoming more dissatisfied with the end result. Isn't it ultimately the woman's choice as to who she decides to sleep with? Why don't these shows talk about making smart choices in the dating arena? How about upgrading yourself? Well ladies, that's what I'm here for.

In your profiles, it's cool to mention your children. In fact, it's best that you indicate you have children and maybe have a photo album dedicated to them. While it's important not to neglect mentioning

---

[1] Nasheed, Tariq. "Why So Many Black Women are Overweight." Mack Lessons Radio Podcast, #50 (2007): http://www.macklessonsradio.com

your kids, it is equally important not to overdo it. I've seen profiles where the main picture is a 3 year old boy, yet the stats show that it is a 28 year old female. There are also other profiles I've seen where women will post 40 pictures of her kids, but have only a couple of herself. Moreover, I've seen other pages with a Sesame Street or Dora the Explorer layout. Men will not take you seriously if your page is riddled with child's play. Plus, if he sees more pictures of little Johnny than you, that sends the message that you might not have any time for him in the first place. Remember, your primary goal is to have the man get to know *you* first.

### Divorce and other Bad Experiences

Over time, we all get a little jaded. Most of us have dealt with trifling people—lying and cheating men, the most popular of the "trifes." You do not have any control over your past. However, you have total control over how you deal with that past. If a former boyfriend or ex-husband cheated on you, do not bring that into a future relationship. If you've been abused, do not assume that all men are that way.

Before you embark on a future relationship with a *Mr. Right* you should "get your mind right" so you do not unintentionally sabotage a potentially good relationship. Read, attend support groups, and develop healthy friendships with women who've had success in these areas.

## PHOTOS

### Number of photos

As I mentioned previously, having too few photos is a bad thing. Even the most wholesome *Mr. Right* wants to see how you look, from head to toe. Yet too many pictures can be a bad thing as well.

It's no secret that women, especially college-aged women, love attention. New York Times Best-Selling Author, Tariq Nasheed has spent a lot of time breaking down the dubbed "Attention Whore Phase," which typically strikes women between the ages of 18 and 21. This phase is described as the psychological rush women experience when getting attention from men. This is no myth. If you pay attention when you go to an 18+ dance party, you will see at least 3 groups of women (if not more) grinding on each other, while thirsty-looking guys are gawking at them. This is a classic example of an attention whore.

"Attention-whoredom" also exists on MySpace as well. A large number of young girls under 21 are constantly posting bulletins or sending notes practically begging guys to comment on their pictures. Usually these women have over 100 photos all over their pages with at least a couple dozen albums. Yet, many ladies fail to realize that this is both unproductive and can actually hurt your prospects.

An eligible guy might spot something undesirable in one of your pictures. Many men have pet peeves. The more photos you have, the more likely he is to spot something he does not like. Plus this behavior of "just wanting to be seen" is unattractive to many grown men. It's time to grow up, unless all you truly want is attention. (Otherwise, why would you be reading this book?) So what's a good number of photos to post? Try to stay between five and twenty.

### Poses

You should also be mindful of how you pose in your pictures. Unless you are a freak and want to let the world know, it is best to delete all the bend over shots in your thong. If you want a respectful guy, then you must present yourself as a woman worthy of respect. I cannot tell you how many females have nothing but breasts and booty all in their picture gallery, but have a nerve to complain about men who objectify them.

There are also some immature, young girl poses, most of which are done by 15-17 year olds, but are sometimes emulated by older women. These include putting a hand on the hip and sticking out your butt to one side. Do not do these. While you might think it's cute, you will only attract immature men. And it is not lady like!

### Clothing

Similar to your poses, do not show off your lingerie collection if you do not want men to assume you are a freak. What amazes me the most is some of the most scantily-clad women verbally demand the most respect in their profiles. Ladies, *do not* be this type of female. Look at things realistically. Again, you attract who you are.

### Overall Photo Quality

Whatever you do, invest in a decent digital camera that's at least 5 Megapixels. It is relatively cheap to take good photos so stop relying on blurry camera phones for your profile photos.

## OTHER THINGS TO KEEP IN MIND

### Friends

If you are a quality woman, try not to have your "crackhead" friends and other "undesirables" on your top friends or in your comments section. Your friends are a reflection of you. Keep that in mind and choose wisely.

### Graphics

Ladies, men are visual creatures. Try to give him the essence of who you are by the theme and layout of your page. If you're a party girl, have a party theme and incorporate some hip hop or dance music. My suggestion is to go to a layout site, such as pimp-my-profile.com, freeweblayouts.net or lovemyflash.com and select a ready-made profile that caters to your creative side. Do not overdo it with the extra glitter graphics and animation. Less is more. At the end of the day, this does little to impress men.

### Intro section

Again, men are visual creatures. Keep in mind that the majority of men (especially *Mr. Right Now*) will pay little if any attention to what you write on your page. For that reason, keep it short and simple. There is no need to post your biography online. Chances are it will not be read, especially if it looks like a term paper!

### Your attitude

To get the best results on the internet (and with life in general), check your ego at the door. There are way too many women online who think they are "flyer" (prettier, more intelligent, etc) than what they really are. Just like with "internet models," there are too many females who are in a fantasy world. Unfortunately, I place a majority of the blame on the barrage of men who flood women with compliments online, which I addressed to a large extent in *The Men's Guide.*

Do not be like this. And on that note, do not fall into the trap of asking men to comment on your photos to build your ego and self-esteem. Your confidence should come from *within*. On the flipside, if someone you do not desire approaches you in a respectful way, you can respectfully decline. Don't be a bitch if someone is genuine with you. I am a firm believer in karma. (If they persist and begin to act "stalkerish," I will give you tips on how to handle this in Chapter 9).

## In conclusion

Overall, stay true to who you are but remain mindful of who you are trying to attract. Keep your page simple, but tasteful. Keep yourself groomed and properly dressed. Physically, be in shape and work on your outward appearance as well as your inner thoughts and emotions. Internally, be real genuine and down to earth. Ladies, remember: if you seriously want a quality guy, you must be a quality lady, first.

# Chapter Two – Sifting Through Men

T his chapter is vital to all women, regardless of the location where you encounter these men. This chapter alone may save you tons of grief and aggravation. In fact, I strongly suggest that each and every lady who is reading this book to go out and purchase, "Play or Be Played" by Tariq Nasheed as it gets even deeper into breaking down the psychology of men for the female audience.

In addition ladies, I want to see that each and every one of you "wins." As they say in the lifestyle of Pimpin', it's the woman who always does the "choosing." In other words, it is the prostitute who ultimately chooses the pimp she will be with. The same holds true in the world of dating. Generally speaking, a woman on top of her game has the final say as to who she chooses to be with. So ladies, now that you've upgraded yourselves and your profiles according to chapter 1, you *must* choose carefully. There are way too many traps you can fall into if you are reckless with the guys you choose to associate yourself with.

Similar to *The Men's Guide*, I will group your male prospects into three categories: Green, Yellow and Red. The "Green" men are the men you go for, the "Yellow" men are the guys you should exercise a good degree of caution with, and the "Red" men are the guys you should run away from.

## RED: Men to Avoid

### Thugs and Criminals

I don't care how "cute" he is or how he makes you feel, messing with a true thug is never a good way to go. Many females are attracted to the "bad boy" quality in thugs, but yet will try to eventually mold him into the man that she wants. However, it never works out this way. If a man wants to sell drugs and rob liquor stores for a living, there is nothing you can say or do to persuade him to do otherwise. As I will explain further in Chapter 7, attempting to change a man on any level will only leave you frustrated and bitter. In addition, messing with thugs is simply outright dangerous. Most thugs are no strangers to violence, disease, incarceration and other thug females. And ladies, no man is worth getting a *pat down*, a *scuff down* or a *beat down*.

Here are some signs you might be dealing with a MySpace Thug:

1. He is totin' a weapon in his photos.

2. He has gangsta rap songs on his page or belongs to a gangsta "clique".

3. Gang tattoos or brandings.

4. He has an all red or all blue theme on his page.

5. His lips are black (weed smoker).

6. He is throwing up gang signs.

7. Every last one of his pictures resembles a mug shot.

8. Even his female friends look like men.

9. All of his friends go by nicknames, like "Smoke" or "Gloc 12".

10. He has a youtube video that he and his "goons" filmed in the hood talking about beating someone down.

### Liars

Ladies, you may think this one is obvious. And the funny thing is, you normally *know* instinctively when a man is lying to you. After all, most men do not lie very well. He may stutter, avoid direct eye contact, act extra defensive, randomly accuse you of things, etc. The most common lies men tell are dumb lies. These are the types of lies he tells simply because he is in the routine of lying. For instance if he is driving somewhere and you ask what he's doing, he may say that he's at home.

Yet many of you choose to ignore or dismiss his lies. This almost certainly will bring you nothing but heartache down the road, even with a fling. If he lies about "dumb stuff," there's no telling what he might potentially keep from you.

Here are some signs his pants are on fire:

1.  His income says over $250,000 (Most people who earn this much, omit this field altogether).
2.  He has a photo with himself holding a stack of ones.
3.  He takes pictures at a car show or dealership, pretending that he actually owns one of these cars.
4.  Claims to know the celebrities in his top friends list.
5.  He elaborates too much on a hard to believe story (liars unconsciously tend to over-explain themselves).

### Non-true-to-the-game Players/Cheaters

What exactly *is* a "Non-true-to-the-game Player"? This is basically a deceptive player: a guy who dates and/or sleeps with multiple women and leads one or more of them to believe his is exclusively dating her. These guys are known for giving women the "I love you" pitch. He will go out of his way to convince you that he is a one-woman man who would never dare cheat on you. He may take you out to eat and give you flowers all in an attempt to win you over. This is the type of guy who will not hesitate to cheat on his girlfriend or wife because he places the *na-na* (the woman's private parts) on a pedestal.

Not only is this deceptive behavior—it's dangerous. Many of these guys have the potential to be reckless as I will explain a little more in a second.

Here are some signs he is a no good, dirty dog:

1. He's done it before (he'll likely do it again).
2. He exhibits any of the signs of a liar.
3. He dismisses all of the females in his photos as "friends" or cousins that he's never been intimate with.
4. He confesses his feelings for you too soon.
5. His notes to you seem rehearsed and too general.
6. He's ultra-secretive about his activities when he's not with you.
7. His relationship status field on his profile changes constantly.

### Reckless Men

A reckless man is the type of guy who always seems to get into bad situations. Trouble always seems to find him. He constantly needs to be bailed out of jail. He always needs money. And this type of careless behavior makes him more likely to lie, cheat and possibly contract diseases.

For the latter reason, this is the type of man you should avoid at all costs as he can literally *kill you*. As reported by various entities such as the University of Southern California, the fastest growing demographic of HIV-infected persons are women between the ages of 15 and 24—specifically Black women.[2] Though it can be argued who deserves the most blame, it cannot be disputed that carelessness, or at least naivety, plays a large role on the part of the women at risk. Whether you are able to identify a reckless man or not, you should *never* engage in unprotected sex with a guy you have not known for a while. Regardless of what he might say or how you feel, only you are ultimately responsible for your safety.

Here are some signs you might be staring at the profile of a "DMX":

---

[2] Jauriqui, Veronica. "Conference Explores HIV Prevention". USC News. 12/44/07. http://www.usc.edu/uscnews/stories/14623.html.

1. His photos show him in compromising situations or breaking the law (e.g. smoking weed, playing with guns).
2. During your message exchanges, he reveals fetishes which show that he might be prone to or might have already broken the law or put him at risk for a disease.
3. He shows signs of hopelessness or outright rebellion (e.g. "Fuck the World" signs on his page, anti-government symbols, self-mutilation tendencies).

### Multiple Baby Daddy Dudes (2 or more Baby's Mothers)

Unfortunately, there is a subset of men who irresponsibly impregnate women but do not raise their children. These are your men who occupy daytime talk shows like Maury Povich and court reality television shows, claiming not to be the father. This is never excusable. Yet, let me have a heart-to-heart with you ladies.

■■■■■■■■■■■■■■■■■■■■■■■■■■■■■■■■■■■■■■■■■■■■■■■■■■■■■■■■

As a side note, there is no need to be his next "BM" (baby momma). Right now there exists a single mother epidemic, most notably in the United States. As much as society comes down on irresponsible fathers who are absent from their children's lives, some culpability belongs to mothers, as well. As explained in chapter one, women are the ultimate "choosers" in all male to female interactions in the Western world. In any relationship, the woman has the final say in whether she chooses to date or be intimate with any man. In terms of sex, men have only one method of birth control aside from abstinence and a vasectomy—the male condom.

On the other hand, there are roughly twelve forms of birth control on the market for women, before and after contraception. In addition, many women have an idea when they are most fertile in their cycles. (There are a variety of fertility tests out there, too). Although these men may be skilled at pulling the wool over your eyes, you would have to be a fool to be his next "victim," especially if he has a history of increasing the world population. So to all the *Mr. Right*-seekers, *run* from these guys as quickly as your pumps will take you. If you are a *Mr. Right Now*-seeker I recommend not even looking in his direction. You can do so much better. The words, "he got me pregnant" should be stricken from your vocabulary. Ladies, the power is in your hands.

■■■■■■■■■■■■■■■■■■■■■■■■■■■■■■■■■■■■■■■■■■■■■■■■■■■■■■■■■■■

There's really no trickery in identifying a guy like this. Chances are if he is the broke and "goaless" type or reckless, he is at risk for having quite a few children from a variety of women.

### Insecure men

I'm sure all of you know what it's like to be with an insecure man. These are normally your possessive, jealous, and your low self-esteem types. He's the type of guy that has to know where you are at all times. He's also the type who will brag to you and everyone else about the latest gadget he purchased or how many cars he owns. In other words, he uses material things to overcompensate for his low self-esteem.

Your danger here is that he will ultimately smother you by constantly second guessing your whereabouts. Most often, these are men who have trust issues due to a previous relationship. When you start to see signs of insecurity ladies, run!

Here are the signs you are looking at the profile of an insecure man:

1. He plays up on his possessions (e.g. He's holding stacks of money or brags about his material possessions).
2. Every single picture shows him with a different female.

3. He exudes any of the characteristics of a thug, yet he lives in an affluent community.
4. He's short (this makes a lot of men insecure).
5. He exudes any of the characteristics of a liar, specifically when it comes to making himself appear wealthier.

## Perverted Men

This is the type of man who owns a set of binoculars to peer into a neighbor's window. He may also be the type to own multiple subscriptions to porn sites. Ladies, I can speak from experience—I used to be *extremely* perverted when I was younger, as most guys are at one point or another. Yet, most men should grow out of this as they become more sexually experienced. However, you always have a few who never seem to grow out of it.

Here are some signs you might have met the real life version Beavis or Butthead:

1. Porn stars in his top friends.
2. Overt or covert references to porn on his page and in message exchanges.
3. He shows signs of inexperience (many inexperienced dudes are perverted, by nature due to their lack of female interaction).
4. He's under 21 (most young men have perverted tendencies).
5. He reveals to you that he owns and uses a webcam.

## Cornballs and "Kissasses"

On MySpace and many other social networking sites, there are millions of guys who go overboard in their ways to get females' attention. Most of these ways involve silly or outright stupid and/or subservient behavior. The "cornball game" is done mostly through picture comments because these guys are too scared to send you a real message. If he does send you a message, it is the type of note that you laugh at and send to your girlfriends as a joke. These guys cannot be taken seriously, since they do not take themselves seriously.

You should avoid cornballs because most of them are not genuine. They are usually guys who get no results with women—and a sexually frustrated man will do some off-the-wall things. Therefore the line between Cornballs, Perverts and "Tricks" (which I will get to in a moment) is blurred. Do you really want to be around a guy who feels he has to act out of character just to get your attention?

This is the easiest man to spot in the red category. Why? Because he is the one leaving comments and messages, similar to the following (and yes, I've seen all of these...and worse):

*-I would spend my entire paycheck on you, but I don't get paid until Friday.*

*-Let's get married today!*

*-I'm good for that body like milk!*

*-Baby come sit on my face. I can give you pleasure that you wouldn't believe!*

### Broke, "Goaless" Men

Ladies, do not get with broke men, especially if you are looking for *Mr. Right*. I am not suggesting that you should leech off someone who is financially stable, but you should always strive to get a man of a higher caliber. Otherwise, you will send yourself an unconscious message that you do not deserve any better. Plus, you will eventually lose respect for the man you are dealing with.

"In a relationship of any kind, if one person feels the other person isn't bringing anything to the table, he or she will begin to disrespect that person." [3] I will speak more about finding someone *with* financial stability later in the chapter.

---

[3] Argov, Sherry. "Keeping Your Pink Slip." Why Men Love Bitches. (2004), Page 181.

Here are some signs that you are looking at the profile of a broke dude:

1. He over-exaggerates his possessions (he's obviously insecure about what he has and is overcompensating).
2. He's over 25, has not yet graduated college and still lives with his mom.
3. He has a ragged or scruffy appearance.
4. He claims to love big girls (usually because he cannot do any better).
5. He has broke friends who share the same qualities.

### Tricks

A "trick" is simply a term for men who attempt to exchange something of value in hopes of receiving sexual gratification. Historically, "trick" has been synonymous with a "john" or a customer of a prostitute. In more modern day terms, one can simply be labeled a trick if he buys a woman he doesn't know a drink. I know many of you may not see the harm in doing this. After all if he wants to treat you to a drink, then you should accept it, right? Wrong.

The problem with tricks is that they *always* expect something in return, even if they don't admit to it. You might *think* something is free, but is it really worth picking up a new stalker? To put it plainly ladies, any man who doesn't know you, yet goes out of his way to use his finances or possessions to impress you is a trick. This means that he wants to get your "goodies".

What does it say about you if you willingly accept gifts knowing what the guy is really after? If you "put out" that makes you a ho, by definition. If you do not give him sex and intend on keeping his gifts, you will ultimately pay in the end. Most "tricks" do not have any *real* money. These are the guys who take out a line of credit or use their rent money to buy bottles for everyone at the club. So what makes you think that he is going to leave you alone after he buys you a diamond necklace or even a drink?  Instead, if you would like to learn about meeting financially stable men, keep reading.

Here are some signs you are looking at the profile of a trick:

1. His page is riddled with images of money, cars and girls.
2. He is in one or more pictures with a stack of dollars in his hands.
3. He puts that he earns over $250,000.00 per year.
4. He has strippers on his top friends list.
5. (In a note) He offers to do something for you like take you out or buy you a gift before you've said anything to him.

### Men on the "Down Low" (Undercover gay men)

Let me start off by saying that I disagree with the mainstream's view that the "down low epidemic" is limited to black men.  This problem spans all communities, cultures and ethnicities.  Many priests, politicians, intellectuals and thugs alike have been found to be closet homosexuals.

This is not an affront to gay men—I personally have no problem with the gay community.  Yet, what I do not respect is someone who pretends to be something they are not, especially in a relationship.  You should always be honest with the person(s) you choose to deal with.  The minute a bisexual or gay man chooses to have sex with a woman who does not know of his *gay ways* is being deceptive.  These men also belong in the reckless category since it is partly to blame for the skyrocketing AIDS rates across the world:

Here are some signs he may be a little *too* sweet:

1. His male friends are feminine looking.
2. He reveals in conversation that he wears makeup, gets his nails painted, his eyebrows arched or his hair *done* (versus getting his hair *cut*).

3. His page is feminine-looking.
4. He idolizes gay and older female entertainers.
5. He is almost *too* fashionable.
6. His hair looks better than yours.

## YELLOW: Use Caution

### *Big Men*

Overall, there is nothing necessarily wrong if you have a preference for larger, huskier men. Unlike women who are primarily judged on their beauty and outward appearances, men are generally more valued based on their finances, attitude and overall sense of style. However, the reason why big men are in the "yellow" category is because this could be the sign of a "larger" issue.

Some men come from families where everyone is big. Mom is large. Dad is large. Uncles, aunts and cousins are large, etc. That is somewhat understandable. However, his weight could be a sign of lack of discipline or outright laziness. Is he broke? Does he have goals in life? What is his workout regimen? You do not need to completely dismiss a larger man—but just put him under a microscope and see what contributed to his weight.

There's no need to break down how to identify a big man, since men do not normally hide their largeness very well. If you go to his photo album or gallery it is usually quite evident.

### *Short Men*

As with larger men, there is no need to dismiss a man based on his height alone. However, you should place a "shorty" under a microscope to see if he has fallen victim to the infamous *Napoleon Complex*. This is defined as "the condition of being small in stature but aggressively ambitious and seeking absolute control."[4] Quite often, I've noticed that a few men under 5'8 are muscular and appear to work out often. This may be due to his attempt to either consciously or subconsciously try to make up for his height. This is not a bad thing. However, if you find that he is exuding signs of a possessive man, take cover and put him into the "red" category.

To identify a short man, look at his height or simply ask how tall he is. If he's a smaller guy, observe him to see if he's showing any signs of an insecure man, as explained earlier in the chapter.

### (True to the Game) Players

Unlike a *Non*-true to the Game Player, a True to the Game Player is a guy who is truthful about his promiscuity. He is secure with himself and knows that females will be down for him, regardless of his dealings with other females. This is the type of man who will never lead you astray and tells the truth about his feelings for you (or lack thereof). He places importance on integrity and looks down on Non-true to the Game Players. In fact, it is his honesty that turns most women on. He is usually extremely well-groomed, has pictures with cute women, has cute females vying for his attention on his comment board or guestbook and has various picture comments from other females. If you're looking for *Mr. Right Now*, this is your man. If you're looking for *Mr. Right*, leave him alone.

In fact, yours truly is this type—as are many of my friends. But this is the type of man that knows he must go through his "player stage"[5]: a phase in a young man's life where he has the biological and psychological need to date and be sexual with as many women as possible. With that said, never try to change a *Mr. Right Now*

---

[4] "Napoleon Complex." Webster's New Millennium™ Dictionary of English, Preview Edition (v 0.9.7). Copyright © 2003-2008 Dictionary.com, LLC.

[5] Nasheed, Tariq. "The Player Stage" Mack Lessons Radio Podcast, #4 (2007): http://www.macklessonsradio.com

into a *Mr. Right*. I lost count of the dozens of females I've run into who are trying to change this kind of guy into "husband material". You cannot change a rolling stone into a mountain, ladies. Trying will only leave you bitter, jaded and depressed.

However, if you are totally cool with a *Mr. Right Now*, without holding any expectations of changing him into a future husband, this is *your guy* (for now). Here are some signs he's a True-to-the-Game Player:

1. He makes it clear that he's "not looking for a relationship".
2. He never denies being intimate with other females.
3. He has a few photos with very attractive women on his page.
4. Women flood his page with compliments and idle chatter.
5. He exudes confidence and smoothness at all times.

\*To know exactly how to find a True to the Game Player, go to www.MySpaceToMyPlace.com and purchase *The Men's Guide* and see how he operates.

\*\*Word of Caution: make sure he's not "reckless". It is important to keep in mind whether or not uses protection during all of his encounters. Moreover, try to do some research into the other females he associates himself with. Are they upstanding individuals or are they thuggets? Be careful—you don't want to catch a beatdown from "Big Sheila" on your way home from work if your fling happens to have a fetish for thug women.

### Men with Children (2 or less baby's mothers)

You may or may not prefer a man with children. While this may be a plus for you if you already have a child, it can also wreak havoc. I have heard many stories of the "other woman" getting involved in her baby's father's relationships. Many times, the man welcomes the baby's mother's interference on a covert level. There is a psychological phenomenon where some people subconsciously enjoy and "get off on" being disrespected. While these men might appear distressed by the verbal abuse, they may also find it internally comforting and even sexually gratifying. This is known as *sadomasochism*.

For this reason, I advise all *Mr. Right*-seekers to be very cautious around men with children. But if you are looking for a *Mr. Right Now* this might be the perfect guy for you. Just make sure no one is following you.

There is no list of ways to tell if a man has a child. No man *should* lie about his status as a father. Just look at his page. On MySpace, look for "Proud Parent" in the "Children" field. And if you are scouting for men, you can elect to search for men with or without children, based on your desires.

### Lovers, Mommas Boys, and "Softies"

In my high school days, I was definitely in this category. I thought that the only way to get a woman was to be nice and sweet 100% of the time. In doing so, I later realized that I appeared weak and spineless. I was also afraid to make brash decisions and worried about her perception of me. I wrote love notes instead of approaching women like a man. In fact, that's why I originally turned to chat lines and eventually the internet—I was too shy to approach women in "real life". I was borderline creepy.

Yet on the flipside, *lover boys* and *softies* can be a big plus. These guys are usually loyal, trustworthy and extremely giving. These are the men who are chivalrous and are there for you until the end. For ladies who desire *Mr. Right*, your man should definitely have some *lover* in him. Yet be careful—if he has no backbone, you may want to back away. (A term in the Player Community for a man with no backbone is a *Simp*).

Signs that he's a lover:

1. Has R&B playing on his profile.
2. Has a romantic theme on his page.
3. Females leaving him comments letting him know that he's "sweet".

Signs that he's a simp:

1. Has simpish songs like "Whatever You Like" by T.I. playing on his page.
2. He says things, like "I don't know...what do you want to do?"
3. Never disagrees with you in a chat and tries to please you *too* much.
4. Leaves you long emails and tells you his life story.
5. Seems like a kiss-ass.

### (Overly) Confident Men

There is a fine line between cockiness and confidence. You obviously want a confident man, ladies. Confidence is sexy and is a good indicator of a man who is going somewhere in life. However, cocky men only care about themselves and therefore do not have the capacity to make you happy—especially a lady seeking *Mr. Right*.

Here are some healthy signs of *confidence*:

1. He shows good posture in his pictures.
2. He appears to be well-rounded with his activities.
3. His first note to you does not seek approval (e.g. "Do you find me attractive?").
4. He is well-groomed in his pictures.

And here are unhealthy signs of *cockiness*:

1. He has a section of his profile talking about what he doesn't like in a girl.

2. He has more than 40 photos of himself (he might be a male attention whore).
3. His status updates say things like "I'm so sexy".
4. He puts out bulletins or requests for people to comment on his photos (another attention whore trait).
5. Kanye West is in his top friends list.

### Long Distance Men

It is never a good idea to engage in any serious dialogue with a man who lives far away, especially if you cannot afford to travel there on a regular basis. In fact, it is a waste of time. (The exception to this is "Vacation Dating" which I will expand on in Chapter 8). It is often said that long distance relationships do not work. Generally I agree. At the very least, it takes an unyielding and strong commitment to make things work.

It's easy identifying a man who lives far away. Most social networking sites prominently display the city and state in each profile. When in doubt, just ask him where he lives. And if you are seeking out men, use the "Browse" or "Find" feature and search for guys within a 10 or 20 mile radius of your zip code.

### Ultra-Religious Men

There is nothing wrong with going to a good Church, Synagogue/Temple, or Mosque and participating in worship. Yet, unless you are a devout follower in his faith, you may want to tread very lightly. Though people wisely tend to stray away from religious topics when first getting to know each other, it is healthy to learn from observing his profile for his level of faith. If your levels do not match with a *Mr. Right*, you may have trouble keeping any semblance of a relationship going.

If you are seeking a *Mr. Right Now*, then this is either a hit or miss. People that are ultra-religious are many times raised in families and environments that cultivate it. Some embrace it while others rebel.

A myth (which I have personally found some validity to) is that the children of preachers (PKs) tend to be some of the most sexually promiscuous people on Earth. This is due to a strict set of behaviors they were raised with and their natural urge to rebel. So while you *Mr. Right Now*-seekers may find a prude in a repressed ultra-religious man, you could quite possibly uncover a beast in the bedroom. Take heed.

Here are some signs you are staring at the profile of Billy Graham's #1 Fan:

1. Jesus pages, evangelists, gospel singers or any other religious figure in his top friends list.
2. Any overt references to God on his page.
3. Church music on his profile page.

### Sexually Inexperienced Men

With the many women I have dealt with over the years, never once did my "lengthy" experience hurt my prospects in getting new women. No female has ever rejected my advances because she knew of my past dealings with various women. On the contrary, I have found that has made women *more* attracted to me once they got wind of my past.

Subconsciously, I believe an experienced man (both in and out of the bedroom) is naturally more confident. He knows he has the capacity to take care of a lady on every level. Predictably, ladies seeking a *Mr. Right Now* should avoid sexually inexperienced men at all costs as he stands little chance in satisfying you. What lady wants to show a man "where to put it"? In addition, he may fall in love with you. If that's not what you are bargaining for, it is probably best to leave these guys alone.

On the flipside, a lady seeking a *Mr. Right* can be *somewhat* open to this type of man especially if she is inexperienced herself. However, I'm warning you *Mr. Right*-seekers to tread lightly as well.

As previously mentioned, most guys need to go through a player stage, beginning sometime in their 20's. If he has not taken the "player plunge" before getting into a relationship with you, you run the risk of being cheated on sometime down the line. And like I'll continue to emphasize throughout this book, *you cannot change him.*

Here are some signs he doesn't know where *it* goes:

1. His conversation with you seems to have no direction.
2. He only sent you a friend request or leaves occasional page comments.
3. He puts up a big front about how many females he's been intimate with, if asked.
4. He exhibits any of the characteristics of a perverted man.

## GREEN: The Men You Want

### Financially Stable/Corporate Men

For the sake of this section, I am defining "financially stable" as someone who makes a decent living: a man who is making at least $45,000 annually to millions, one who may own his primary residence, has a 401(K) and maybe some other investment vehicles. These are your engineers, physicians, counselors, teachers, programmers, managers and even plumbers and electricians. In the upper echelon, you may come across a corporate attorney, middle to large business owner, vice president, director, senior programmer, real estate tycoon, regional or nationally-known entertainer, etc, etc.

The benefits for a man like this can be great and I advise that each of you aim for a man who brings this to the table. After all, you are now an upgraded "fly girl" after putting chapter 1 into practice, right?

Here are some ways to tell if you are staring at the profile of a potential baller:

1. He has celebrities and/or well-to-do people in his top friends and he is in their top friends, as well.
2. Celebrities and/or well-to-do people leaving comments on his wall.
3. He is listed as a college graduate (rather than a student) with a degree in a scientific, mathematical field or a law degree.
4. He in inadvertently reveals that he lives alone and has his own vehicle.
5. On his page, look for interests that include real estate, any national memberships to prestigious clubs, wine tasting, art collecting, etc.
6. He reveals that he comes from *old money*; perhaps that a relative died and left him thousands of dollars, an estate or some sort of death benefit.

*For more tips on where to encounter men offline with some "paper" I highly recommend purchasing *The Art of Golddigging* by Tariq Nasheed.

### Local Men

In contrast with "Long Distance Men" above, you should aim to find either *Mr. Right* or *Mr. Right Now* within 20 miles or at least within 50 miles of your home. Why invest in someone if they need to catch a flight to come see you? It is one thing if you were able to establish a close-proximity relationship and then one of you had to move temporarily. However, it is something entirely different if you are actually starting out over 50 miles apart. Simply put, stick to local men. And if the men in your area are not your taste, move or venture out to other places on weekends.

As explained, use these social networking sites to find men in your area. If you receive a note from a guy, look for his location and react appropriately.

## Mature Men

Maturity should be a *must* in all of your relationships. Even in a non-committed fling, you want to know that the man is mature enough to handle it. His level of discreteness, his ability to satisfy you, and his ability to understand the emotional ramifications all plays into his maturity.

As you have probably observed throughout your own experiences, maturity does not always come with age. There are some forty year old men running around claiming to be rappers and mooching off other people. At the same time, many young men are buying homes and investment before the age of 25. Age is not always the determining factor in maturity.

Here are some signs that you are looking at the profile of a man of wisdom:

1. He uses correct English with very little slang, if any.
2. His top friends include actual people that he knows, rather than celebrities, porn stars, and athletes.
3. He exhibits any of the characteristics of a financially stable man.
4. When he writes you, he sends you a note in complete sentences without slang or extreme grammatical errors.
5. His emails are longer than three words.

## Educated Men

When I say educated, I am not only speaking about men who have graduated with at least a Bachelor's degree from a major college or university. These can also include men who have acquired a viable education elsewhere, like skilled plumbers, actors and even models. Even Microsoft founder, Bill Gates was a college dropout before going on to become one of the richest men in the world.

These men are important if you want someone on your level or at least someone who will help you "upgrade." And more often than not, an educated man is a man who can carry on an interesting conversation.

Here are some signs you might be looking at the profile of a professor:

1. He shows any signs of a financially stable or mature man.
2. He shows a command over the English language in his notes and on his page.
3. He lists more than one book in his "favorite books" section and it does not include a comic book.
4. His friends show the same signs.

### Men who are good in bed

This is a plus for a *Mr. Right*-seeker and a <u>must</u> for a *Mr. Right Now*-seeker. Some women say that size matters. Yet most women would agree that size is not the primary formula for satisfaction in the bedroom. A man must be good, from foreplay through post-orgasmic spooning. All around knowledge and variety in the bedroom is key to a happy sex life so you should feel justified in wanting a man who can perform.

Here are some ways to tell if your man is a gifted performer in the bedroom:

1. His comment section is littered with women hinting that they've already "done the deed." (i.e. "When can I see you again?")
2. A man who appears to exude good sexual energy.
3. A man who is in shape and shows an interest in nutrition. (Shows that he is in tune with his body)

### All around cool men

Above all, aim for all around cool men. Cool combines confidence, intelligence, style, sensitivity and strength. These can also be a combination of any of the "GREEN" men I talked about in this chapter, along with having some of the positive traits in a few of the "YELLOW" men.

# Chapter Three – Showing Interest

**Y**ou might be familiar with the James Brown classic, "It's a man's world." In terms of how the world operates, this holds true, even today. Though the gap is closing, men on average tend to be the top wage earners, if not the principle breadwinners in the household. More men hold executive positions, head countries, and for the 44th time, yet another man is President of the United States.

Yet in the dating game, it is *women* who write the rules. In the animal kingdom, it is the females who actually choose their suitors, not the other way around. The male members of the moose, caribou, the elk and other members of the deer population are known for their mighty antlers. Having antlers is not solely for protection. According to Redlands Daily Facts, antlers are actually an evolutionary way for males to attract females—evidence that it's the personal choice of female deer to choose males.[6]

This is similar in humans. Ladies, you *know* that getting basic sex isn't a problem. For an average or even below average woman, to get sex from a man requires little effort. As I spoke about in *The Men's Guide*, there is no shortage of men who would readily have sex with nearly any female, with little regard for her size, appearance, educational level, and even hygiene. That's why *Mr. Right Now*-seekers literally have their pick over what kind of man they want to "snag."

However, let me warn you ladies. Don't be so quick to project your fantasies onto a man you just met. If he's insincere, this may end up jading you in the long run. I will dig deeper into how to prevent that in Chapter 7.

The point is ladies, it is *you* who chooses. And as that line in Spiderman goes, "with great power comes great responsibility."

---

[6] Seff, Nancy. "Antlers: fancy headgear with more than one purpose." Redlands Daily Facts. 12/18/04. http://www.highbeam.com/doc/1P2-10963958.html.

Take ownership of your choices and choose correctly. Now onto more game.


## SHOWING INTEREST ONLINE

In the "real world," most women tend to be more subtle when choosing a man that peaks her interest. A typical female prefers not to make the first move but may employ tactics such as standing in the proximity of her interest, prolonged eye contact, playing with her hair, flashing a smile, saying hello, or even asking him a general question. This challenges the man to notice your invite and if interested, he will "grow a pair" and approach.


There are three main ways for a lady to properly show interest online without seeming too hungry.

1. Sending a Friend Request or Invite.
2. Leaving a comment on his profile (wall) or on a photo.
3. Sending a message.*


*This should be the *last* resort, particularly for *Mr. Right*-seekers. I will get to that later.


### *Sending a Friend Request or Invite*

This is the primary way I have been able to "uncover" women that are interested in me online. The process is simple. Starting from just about any social networking site's home page, select the "Browse" or "Find Members" feature and enter your search criteria, including your zip code, desired height and weight, education level, kids, etc. Once you find the profile of a man you fancy, click "Invite" or "Add Friend Request."


Lastly, you can also attach a note to most invites or add friend requests. If this guy is someone who's proven himself to be someone who's being sought after (many friends and comments all over his page), this is probably the best way to go. Keep these notes *brief!* Here are some examples of a note you can send along with a friend request attachment:

"Saying hello. :)"

"Nice hat!"

"I really love the music on your page!"

Make sure the note is honest. For instance, do not say that you like his music if you really don't. Pick out something you like and be genuine.

### Leaving a Profile, Wall, or Photo Comment

Leaving a comment is a more elusive and roundabout way to get at a guy online. However, it can be an effective way to get a man's attention. It is best to go with this method if either 1) He's new to MySpace or doesn't have too many comments, and/or 2) you are very attractive. (Be realistic on #2, ladies. When I say *attractive*, I mean that you've received lucrative offers to model in magazines or get approached by financially wealthy men with money on a regular basis. I'm talking less than 1% of the female population. If you want my opinion on your "grade," send me a question and attach your profile link, using my "Ask Flyness" tab on www.MySpaceToMyPlace.com.)

Leaving a comment is simple and you may follow the same format as the friend request notes. A simple, "hello" or "loving the music" is sufficient. You may also go to one of the MySpace design pages, like Freeweblayouts.net and paste a pre-made HTML graphic on his bulletin or wall.

### Sending a Message

I am cringing at the idea that some of you ladies might prefer this method. Except for extraordinary circumstances (which I will get to in a moment), I advise against it. Too many ladies immediately lose their *value* when they choose to go this route. Some notes I get are similar to "Damn baby, you're cute." While I normally reply, it is just to thank them and I usually do not give it a second thought. It's hard to take a woman seriously who makes herself seem *too* easy or available. I don't care how cute he is, you should be somewhat of a challenge...especially in the beginning.

In addition, sending the first message eliminates finding out whether he's "man enough" to approach you. Do you really want a guy that you have to call the shots with? If that's the case, why not date another woman? Making it *too easy* increases the likelihood that you might be talking to an ultra-shy guy or a borderline geek. And there are plenty of geeks to go around online. The computer is a geek's paradise. The only time I recommend sending him a message is if he has over 1000 friends or does not come online very often. (On most sites you can look for "last login" to see when he last signed in.) And again, if you think he's the type that gets bombarded with friend requests and comments, a message might be best.

If you must go the message route, find something about him that you genuinely like and give him a quick compliment or comment. If you have a quick question about him, feel free to ask. Do not be overtly sexual or flirty. Here are some examples of what to say in a message, in addition to the friend request notes and comments suggested above:

-I love that layout on your page. Where did you get it from?

-I like your smile. How's life treating you in Las Vegas?

-I've never heard that song on your page. Any idea what album that's on?

-That shirt looks good on you. Where do you shop?

### *Then What?*

If he's truly interested *and* if he has enough courage and charisma to reply back, he will. If neither is true, you will not receive a reply. (That of course, is not to mean that every reply means he's genuinely interested.) If you do not receive a reply, move on. Do not keep sending requests and saying "hi" if he is not reciprocating. On a weekly and sometimes daily basis, the same females write me time and time again attempting to get my attention. (Although I am very busy and might have missed your first attempt, this makes you look desperate.) Save your humility. Simply move on if he doesn't reply.

If he replies, let the dialogue flow. If you read *The Men's Guide* you will notice how a real man is supposed to conduct a dialogue online. Your dialogue *should* be long enough to learn about him and feel comfortable, but not so long that you are having idle chatter. If you find that he has trouble "closing the deal" you can either politely excuse yourself and end the interaction or you can help him out with a simple: "Call me 555-5555." That said, I will go into all of the safety precautions you must take heed to in Chapter 9, including making sure you are not picking up a new stalker.

*Here are some more* **Do NOTs** *of message sending:*

-Do not comment on his car or his home or he may take you for a golddigger.

-Do not express outright interest—this lowers your value and he will take you for granted. (Everyone likes a challenge)

-Do not come across as being too sarcastic too soon, if you are interested. Keep in mind that it's not as easy to pick up on sarcasm online, as it is in person. If you cannot help yourself, use *emoticons* or "smiley faces." Refer to the "Emoticon Glossary" at the end of the book for a quick guide.

# Chapter Four – Conversation Skills

M uch of my last book was dedicated to conversation flow, including the last chapter which contained actual chats I have had with women I met online. As you have probably noticed, there are too many guys who lack the ability to converse properly. However, I have also witnessed many women who need some help as well. Although, I will be providing chat examples, this chapter is dedicated to the fundaments of how to conduct a message exchange or chat.

## MESSAGE EXCHANGING AND SENDING NOTES

At this point you have either shown interest or reciprocated interest and your "prospect" has proven to be receptive. Now we are at the message exchange. Here are some general rules.

1. Don't assume he's an angel.
2. Don't assume he's the devil.
3. Do not push the envelope when it comes to topics and language.
4. Be gentle, yet straightforward.
5. Don't drag it out.

### *Don't assume he's an angel*

This is every guys' dream—especially a player looking to hit it "with the quickness." It is a well-known player rule to try to "tap draws" with a female within a few days of meeting. This is because too many women assume that the twinkle in his eye, his voice, his scent, and the way he makes you feel means that he's a keeper. I really can't blame the players for this one—many of you women *know* deep down the type of guy you are messing with. Yet, your emotions usually always take control and master players (like myself) know how to take advantage of this. However, True to the Game Players will keep it real with you when they see that you are developing feelings. *Non*-True to the Game Players will exploit this and may have you going for months, thinking that you are in a relationship. All the while, he is out there getting ass on the side and repeating the formula with one or more females. The intuition of a woman is strong. Trust your gut, use your head and do not be so quick to project your fantasies onto a guy you don't know. I'm not necessarily saying don't sleep with him quickly—but be realistic in terms of the type of man he is and what you desire from him. Point blank—you cannot change any type of player into "hubby material" by sexing his brains out.

So in a message exchange, try to look behind his words. Don't be overly excited if you two happen to share the same hobbies, tastes in movies or other things. Stay neutral and level-headed. Go with the vibe but also stay realistic and be sure to convey this in your messages. For instance, lets say you discover you share the same birthday.

How NOT to handle it:

*You: So when's your birthday?*

*Him: February 23*

*You: Me too! OMG, wow! That's so crazy! :-P*

How to handle it:

*You: So when's your birthday?*

*Him: February 23*

*You: Interesting...mine too :)*

By remaining cool, but interested (the smiley face accomplishes still seeming interested) you are helping to build healthy emotional and sexual tension that might carry on into a possible date down the line.

### Don't assume he's the devil

On a similar note, do not assume that he is the devil, either. I can spot an insecure woman the moment she blurts something out of her mouth. Sometimes you can tell in her pictures if she's the type that will challenge any and every guy who's nice to her. Women like this are the ones who've been through some drama in their lives—so much in fact, that she subconsciously carries it into all of her relationships. This will drive quality men away and leave you with men who also need drama in their lives. This will leave you in a vicious cycle of unhappiness and bitterness. As hard as it may be, try to treat each new guy as a new guy. While it's good to learn from past experiences, don't let them sabotage the present.

In a message exchange do not insinuate or assume he's a player, liar, or cheater unless you have concrete evidence (based on the indicators mentioned in Chapter 2). Not all men cheat, nor do all men lie. If you find that the majority of your ex-boyfriends fit this description, perhaps you should re-examine what draws you to these types of men.

### Do not "push the envelope" too much

This is mainly a message for my *Mr. Right Now*-seekers. Some of you ladies reading this book are extremely freaky. There are some women I have met, both on and offline, who've completely *blown my mind* (and I mean that). I have chatted with females who not only bring up sex, but divulge into topics like oral sex techniques, my "size," pornography, anal sex, vibrators, etc. etc. This sometimes happens within a minute or two after the first "hello!"

As freaky you might be or as flirty as you are, pushing it *too much* gives the guy a reason to see you as a walking vagina. No matter how much you might like strange penis in your life, every normal person wants to feel respected. You are throwing it out of the window when you push that too soon. And say you two decide to meet—he has no reason to think that you are anything less than a *"complete slide,"* AKA a mindless girl to have sex with. (For those of you who have high sex drives, that's fine. Just let him discover that on his own *after* the first chat with him.) So in a message exchange be cool and don't be so quick to tell him about your dildo collection, deluxe pornography set, and that dominatrix cage in your bedroom.

### Be gentle, yet straightforward

Some guys just "don't get it." This is why you must try to be clear with your intentions. For example, let's say you and a guy are engaged in a message exchange. Midway into your exchange, he says something that turns you off or you feel yourself losing interest for some reason. Most sensible guys will take a clue and move on. However, some men will persist in writing you continuously. If you try to ignore a man, he may write you multiple times per day, hoping to "win" you back. If you block him, he may use another account to write you. This is why it's important to remain straightforward with these men. Here are some examples of what to say when you are no longer interested in someone online:

### The Quick and Easy Exit

"You seem cool, but I am not interested. It was nice meeting you."

### The "What You Said" Exit

"I'm not really cool with [what you said/did/suggested] and don't think we're on the same page. It was nice meeting you but this isn't working out. Take care."

### The Boyfriend Exit

"I'm sorry, but I have a boyfriend. You're nice, but I don't think he would be cool with where this is going. It was nice meeting you."

All three of these examples were both gentle and to the point. Keep that in mind when dealing with someone in an exchange, especially if they're "hard-headed." If by chance he persists after that, don't worry. In Chapter 9, I will go deep into the subject of both avoiding and handling more serious problems.

### Don't drag it out

I was definitely guilty of this in my younger days. Though I place the primary focus of conversation flow on the man, ladies have some control as well. While the man may "drive the car" in a conversation, the woman has a hand on the wheel, her foot on the brake and has reign over the traffic signals. Simply put, if your message exchange has spanned more than a week and/or has exceeded ten exchanges, you two are in violation of WASTING TIME. Honestly, what is the point in having a cyber-relationship? Your time would be better spent in the library or at the gym. As mentioned in Chapter 3, once you guys are reduced to idle chatter you should either end the interaction or leave your number. Any man who lets it get to the point of idle chatter is not a skilled conversationalist and needs help. Act appropriately.

*A key sign that you are caught up in idle chatter is if you receive a note saying, "So what are you doing?"

## HANDLING CHATS

Initially, most social networking interactions begin with a message exchange. If it progresses, sometimes it goes right to the phone. Other times, it will go into a chat. Chances are if the message exchange is going in rapid succession (because you two may be online), then it might be easier to switch to a chat first. In the chat session, keep the same principles mentioned above in mind. Do not assume he's the perfect man or a man from hell. Don't push the conversation too hard, be open and direct, and lastly, don't drag it out.

In addition, there are some more things to keep in mind. If you are fully engaged in a chat with him and he is slow to reply or keeps sentences too brief, he is very likely chatting with at least one other female. Men tend to be horrible multitaskers. There is no real need to point this out to him. However, this is something you must keep in mind, especially if you are considering him for a *Mr. Right* position. He is probably not your best candidate.

On the flip side, let's say you are truly interested but you are in an area of poor reception, at your job, or busy with another pressing matter. Instead of taking two minutes to write a reply that would otherwise take ten seconds, let him know and give the guy the option to hang on. Else exchange numbers. If you're not clear, he will assume that you are not interested, rather than just busy.

## SHOULD YOU HELP HIM TRANSITION TO THE PHONE?

I am personally not a fan of women helping "softies" with their game. Chances are, if you have noticed that the guy you are exchanging messages with is having trouble "closing the deal" or moving it to the phone, then he's a "softy." Though he might be the sweetest guy in the world, the average lady finds it difficult to become sexually attracted to a softy. Do not apologize for feeling this way—it is not masculine. This is the same type of guy who plays the "so what do you want to do" game, for example:

You: "So what do you want to do?"

Him: "I don't know....what do you want to do?"

If you encounter a man like this, he is probably not worth keeping around—especially if you seek a *Mr. Right Now.* (If he can't even tell you what he wants, there is little chance that he can *give* you what you want in the bedroom).

But what if you want to give him a chance? What if he's a superior, upstanding guy with a good head on his shoulders, very attractive, but yet has trouble suggesting that you two take the interaction offline?

### Give him a hint

If you think that all he needs is a hint to prevent him from rambling, suggest that you have to go but would love talking to him again. If he suggests speaking online again and you *know* that you two have spoken enough, then its time to move on. He's either not interested *or* he's too shy to move the interaction forward. Either way, next!

### Put (throw) the ball in his court

Simply put, end the message exchange by saying, "Well, I have to go. Take my number." See if he calls. If he doesn't call, he was not interested enough.

### Some more tips

-Try to use correct grammar and avoid funky letter-number substitutions, **LyK3 tH1S**. This mainly applies to young girls. If you're not sure what I am referring to, then don't worry—it is probably not you.

-Do not ramble in a chat. Keep replies and statements thoughtful but not too long. This is draining.

-Do not be too brief in a chat if you are truly interested. He may otherwise be discouraged and may lose interest.

-If you know the chat will never go further, save your time and his. Excuse yourself and move on.

# Chapter Five – Tips on
# the Phone Game

# HISTORY LESSON

*Traditionally it was normally the man who made the phone calls to the woman—especially the first call. Following that, the man would pick up the girl, take her out, and bring her home. Whatever your feelings are about that concept, you've probably figured out that times have certainly changed. Unless you're a gorgeous supermodel, let go of the idea of quality men always making the first phone call.*

*As women from all over are becoming more financially savvy and asserting their independence, many men are adjusting and taking the more laid back approach. Pop culture is ruled by the independent woman. This is the Hillary Clinton and Sarah Palin age. Just look at the theme across a variety of music genres—it seems as if every other song on the radio is an empowering battle cry speaking to the plight of women. Yet, from an experienced player's point of view, many women have let their new found independence go to their heads. (Not you, of course). However, that's just reality and that concludes my "history lesson".*

The reason why I had to "take you to school" is because the paradigm shift of male-female relations has a great impact on the phone number game. The world of social networking is no different. There are a large number of you who have "I don't need a man" themes on your pages, all the way down to how you choose to carry the interaction offline—the phone number. Here are some "Do Nots" that you should take heed to.

## THE DO-NOTS OF THE PHONE NUMBER GAME

1. Do not challenge him, unnecessarily
2. Do not give out fake numbers
3. Do not play phone games

### *Do not challenge him, unnecessarily*

Despite the first few paragraphs in this chapter, many of you are still of the mindset that it's okay to challenge a potential interest. Let me be clear—I am not saying that *being* a challenge is a bad thing. Doing things like keeping him guessing and not always being highly available are key. As I explained earlier, playing it cool and somewhat neutral is your best move in the beginning.

However *challenging* a potential interest is not a good move. The difference between *being* a challenge and being *challenging* is like night and day. For instance, say you're at a club and an attractive man you have been chatting with hands you his card. A woman who's a challenge might accept the card but will not call for at least two or three days, giving off the vibe that she's not "thirsty" for him. Yet a woman who is *challenging* may look at the card and say, "I don't call guys. Why do I have to call you?"

It is the same online. Ladies, if a man offers you his number and you are interested in carrying the interaction forward, give him a call without the combative remarks. As I explained in *The Men's Guide*, a man who gives his number to the woman usually signifies a man who's confident enough to give the woman the power of *choosing* him. Don't blow it.

### *Do not give out fake numbers*

I don't care how short he is. I don't care how much he annoys you. Giving him a fake number—especially online—is a bad move. If you meet a guy in a strange city, *at least* giving him a fake number has no real consequences since the chances of reuniting again are next to zero. But if you are chatting with a man online, what is giving him a fake number going to accomplish? If he is still messaging you after being "gentle, yet straightforward", then a fake number will probably make this "softy" try harder. If the concept is not proving useful in trying to "shake off" a stalker, then Chapter 9 is for you.

## Do not play phone games

Similar to the rule above, do not give him the inkling that your motives are genuine when they really aren't. Be real. If you're not totally interested, do not string a man along by giving him your number. From time to time, I come across females who act extra exasperated when they keep getting phone calls from their exes or "stalkers". Yet in reality, these stalkers were mostly men she initially strung along (or is still stringing along) so she could feel validated. Don't do this. Furthermore, I cannot think of a better waste of time than ignoring phone calls from undesirable men. If you want to test your desirability, enter a swimsuit contest or join a modeling agency. If you want an ego boost, read books on self improvement. Have some integrity in your game and exercise some maturity.

Here are some other popular phone games that you should _never_ resort to:

-Letting him call but having another man answer the phone.*

-Hanging up on him and pretending it was an accident (one of my exes did this to me, plenty of times).

-Putting him on hold for long periods of time.

-Giving him your number but forgetting (or pretending to forget) who he is.

-Pretending to be someone else and telling him that you aren't home or no longer live there.

*Unless the "gentle, but straightforward" approach does not work

## THE DOs OF THE PHONE NUMBER GAME

There are no real "do's" to the phone number game. Just don't screw it up. If you like this guy, try to let go of any baggage from past relationships and bad experiences. Also, do not fall into the trap of playing the types of games listed in the previous section.

Instead, soak up his vibe and feel his unique energy. Sometimes if you just let go, good things will happen on their own.

## CONVERSATIONS GONE WRONG

Sometimes you may not know your stallion is really a donkey, until you speak with him on the phone. Here are some common problems when you find out that *Mr. Right* is actually *Mr. Wrong* on the telephone:

*-He talks too much.*

*-He talks too little.*

*-He forgets important things about you (like your name).*

*-He uses inappropriate language or humor.*

*-He talks about sex too early.*

If he exhibits any of these problems and you no longer wish to continue communicating with him, use the "gentle, but straightforward" approach, similar to the one described in Chapter 4. For example:

> "I have to be honest with you. Although I think you're a good person, I don't feel like we are connecting well on the phone, so I think we should end it. It was nice meeting you but this isn't working out. Take care."

If you just have a bad vibe or wish to end the phone call for any other reason, talk about *chemistry*:

> "I have to be honest with you. Although I think you're a cool guy, I just don't feel any chemistry, so I think we should end

it. It was nice meeting you but this isn't working out. Take care."

Letting him down *early*, *easy* and yet, *earnestly* is the best way to handle a man you truly do not desire. Entertaining a man for a long period of time for the sake of sparing his feelings (or yours) only prolongs the end result—you hurting his feelings. Getting it over with sooner rather than later will prevent him from resenting you and will alleviate a great degree of guilt. Do not resign yourself to giving into his emotions.

## TEXTING

Simply put, try to avoid this method of communicating unless you need to give him some quick information or you are in an area where you cannot talk. Texting as a primary means of communication is a waste of time and energy. Plus it robs you of the opportunity to get to know him, beyond words. It's impossible to get the full "flavor" of what someone is saying in a text message. You might as well have an online, chatroom relationship.

Here are some examples when texting is okay:

-You're in the movies (not on a date), at a play, or at the hairdressers beneath the dryer.

-You're giving him your street address, email address, etc. and want him to get the correct spelling.

-You're giving him a quick message, such as "I got home okay" or "Just saying hello. I had fun last night."

# Chapter Six – First Date Tips

Although the focus of this book is finding quality men online, I would be doing you a disservice by not dedicating at least one chapter to your first date. The reason why this is so important is because first impressions are lasting. How you begin in a relationship is typically how it ends up. That's why it is so important that you start off genuine and on a positive note. It is very difficult to "flip the script" midstream. That said, you cannot change a *Mr. Right Now* into a *Mr. Right* in most cases. (I will discuss this further in Chapter 7).

## BEFORE THE DATE

### *Hygiene and Appearance*

Based on the tips given in Chapter 5, you should be well on your way to a date with a man you desire. Before the date, make sure your hygiene is in order. You would be surprised at how many women *need* to pay careful attention to this. (I apologize to those who are already "on point" with your hygiene). Always shower, moisturize and use deodorant before a date. I highly recommend using baby oil or coconut oil on warm, moist skin coming out of the shower, followed by your favorite lotion. Make sure your hair is neatly styled with minimal split ends. Scarves and headrags are a no-no, unless it is for religious or cultural purposes.

Clothes should also be clean and ironed. Some women do not wash their jeans that often since they tend to fade. At the very least, please make sure they are fresh before putting on. And in the event you are seeking *Mr. Right Now*, make sure your bra and panties match. I have spoken with many females who tell me that this has been the reason they've rejected sex from men—simply because they were in too much of a hurry to find a matching set of bra and panties.

Be sure to look fresh and smell good. Do not go overboard with perfumes. In addition, be careful not to use too much makeup. Don't go nuts with eye shadow and lipstick, especially.

### Safety Precautions

1. Meet in a public place.
2. Let people know where you are.
3. Any date beginning after 9:00PM is a booty call (in most cases).

Typically, it is best to meet in public preferably where people are around. You do not have to make it blatantly obvious and tell him that you want to be in public—just suggest it. A great place for this is the bookstore, coffee shop or even a mall food court. If he suggests meeting somewhere beyond your comfort zone, you might say, "Let's meet at the Starbucks near Main Street. Do you know where that is?" Wherever you go, make sure you are in a public area, in case you didn't do a good job in reading Chapter 2 and ended up with O.J. Simpson's twin brother.

In addition, make sure at least one other person knows where you are and who you're with. Again, in the unlikely event you mistakenly went on a date with The Boston Strangler, it is a good thing for someone to already know your whereabouts that may be able to intervene if something bad should occur. That goes for any date.

Lastly, all *Mr. Right*-seekers should avoid dates beginning after 9:00PM. In most cities, with the exception of New York, Miami, Los Angeles and the like, the number of possible activities declines sharply after 9:00PM. Depending on your city, movie theaters, restaurants, bowling alleys, pool halls, etc. are all closing or beginning to close around this time. Therefore, this leaves sex as one of the few activities left. It really doesn't matter what you say as a disclaimer before or during a date—actions speak louder than words. Unless you want to open the door to "something more," start the date before eight. I will offer you a few more safety tips in Chapter 9.

## DURING THE DATE

### Sizing Him Up

Similar to your first phone call, do not engage in games and immature behavior. Again, if this is a man that you are attracted to, let him know that. Every now and then, hold eye contact. Smile and be polite. If you happen to be shy and have trouble expressing yourself, it's okay to let him know. For instance you may say something like, "I apologize if I'm a little quiet. I'm shy and need to warm up a bit."

If you are seeking a *Mr. Right Now* chances are you will know very early whether he can *get it*, or sleep with you. If you are not looking for a serious commitment and want to size up his physique, give him a warm 2-3 second hug when you meet him. I won't get into specifics, but this is one way to try to determine "what he's working with".

As I stated earlier in the chapter, one of my favorite places to meet women is at the coffee shop. Ice cream shops and bookstores are also ideal. These are great places to relax and usually conversation is facilitated by your surroundings. It's easy to look around and talk about various ice cream or coffee flavors, different books, and transition into various subjects. Having places that are easy for conversation puts you both at ease.

If you sit down facing one another, you will notice how he sits and carries himself. Generally if he slouches or has bad posture, there is something lacking in his life—it may be confidence. Check for eye contact to see if he's shy. Also if he's telling a story, this is a great way to see if he's a liar. As he's speaking, check his eyes. Blinking or lack of eye contact might be an indication that he's not telling the truth. If he looks to his upper-right (your upper-left) as he's telling a story or answers a question, chances are he is lying. We as humans tend to look to this direction which is toward the creative half of our brains—the upper right hand portion. This is a credible way to determine if someone is being truthful with you.[7]

### Who Pays?

As discussed during the History Lesson at the beginning of Chapter 5, times are changing. The man is no longer always the person who pays. Some women are fine with this while others find it completely unacceptable. Personally, this is never an issue for me. Since most of my first dates have taken place at a coffee shop, bookstore, museum or the park, it is rare that I ever spend more than ten dollars. Nonetheless, whether you believe you should pay or not, I ask that you try to remain neutral—especially if you are seeking *Mr. Right*.

Typically if the man asks the woman out, he should pay for it all. If the woman asks the man out, she usually pays half, if not for all of the date. If you believe this man is a keeper you might consider pulling out your wallet or purse and spring for the bill or check without hesitation, if you can afford it. Most secure men will be taken aback by your generosity and will likely "up the ante" and treat you to some place especially nice on the second date. I first heard that idea from author Tariq Nasheed, but it didn't click until a date I went on a few years ago. Not only did this woman pay for the date, but she also gave me a few gifts. Instinctively, I felt very inclined and willing to do more for her, during the next go round.

Nonetheless, there are indeed *some* men who will feel hurt or disrespected if you attempt to pay the tab. He may insist that he pays. If this happens, don't fight it. If he's an older man (above 35) this is understandable. However, if he is under 35 he is probably very insecure. How you handle this type of man is up to

---

[7] Blifaloo.com. "Eye Direction and Lying." Eye Movement and Direction and How it Can Reveal the Truth or a Lie. (2005) http://www.blifaloo.com/info/lies_eyes.php

you.  Yet this type of behavior should be a big red flag if you are seeking *Mr. Right.*

Other than this, have fun on your first date.  However, *Mr. Right*-seekers should be careful about going back to his place or bringing him back to yours.  Unless you want to open the door to the possibility of sex (which might put your *Mr. Right* at risk for only being a *Mr. Right Now*), don't do this.  It is true that you have the legal and moral right to refuse sex at any time, for any reason.  No man should force himself on you.  But it is ultimately your responsibility to think ahead and not allow someone the "space" to assume you might be "down to get down."  However, if you do "get down" and decide to have sex, always make sure he wears a condom.  There's nothing wrong with using a female condom either, so there's never an excuse to have unprotected sex— especially outside of a relationship.  It is simply too dangerous.

## AFTER THE DATE

Following the date, simply be cool.  You may follow up in a couple of days to say hello and test his reaction.  If you are strictly his friend with benefits, keep these phone calls especially short, only shooting the breeze for a couple of minutes and to arrange your second "interaction."  If you are seeking *Mr. Right*, repeat the same conversation rules from the last chapter and do your best to read his actions and words.

# Chapter Seven – Mr. Right or Mr. Right Now?

P rovided you did not skim through the book and happen to land on this page, congratulations on making it to this chapter. I congratulate you because finding *Mr. Right* or *Mr. Right Now* is not only the prevailing theme of the book, but this is one of the most prevailing issues that affect single women in today's age.

I cannot tell you how many women I come across who are unhappy with their dating lives—and ladies, I've heard it all. As a matter of fact, Chapter 2 was created in part, due to the vast conversations I have had with unsatisfied women. More than anything, the force behind this undercurrent of unhappiness is driven by her "underachieving" man being *too nice* or *too "player"*.

In my teenage days I used to wonder why the good girls were both attracted to *and* repelled by the bad boys. I remember being both shocked and fascinated by the degree to which a "non-true-to-the-game" player would manage to sweep women off their feet, having his way with them, and running off like a thief in the night. It never made sense to me.

As a nice guy, I used to sit and listen to these womens' problems and (like most men) hope that she would reward my listening ear with sex and affection…which never worked. Believe me, I tried *many* times. Instead, these women would eventually, and sometimes repeatedly, reward these players with more sex, affection and attention despite being treated like a stray cat. It was almost "animalistic". Yet, like clockwork, these women would predictably come back to me and complain about his cheating and womanizing. After years of being *Mr. Nice Guy*, I grew tired of the pattern and searched for the reasons *why* women seemed to be so confused and dissatisfied.

**These situations gave way to my realization that most of the problems women have are their inability or unwillingness to**

discern between a *Mr. Right* and a *Mr. Right Now* (bold means read it again).

### *Are you <u>unable</u> or <u>unwilling</u>?*

Dissatisfied, single women normally fall into two categories: 1.) **unable** or 2.), **unwilling** to choose between a long term guy and a short-term fling, or a *Mr. Right* versus a *Mr. Right Now*.

Women who are *unable* to tell the difference between the two types of men are much rarer than you think. Unable women are primarily those who are not socially in-tune to the way *Mr. Right Now*'s act. Therefore they are "excused" from bearing most of the blame I place on unwilling women. Unable women include young adults (18 and under), culturally isolated women (such as immigrants), and sheltered women. Once these women are released into the real world, it is only a matter of time before they mistakenly choose the "wrong Mr." and become dissatisfied. If you fit this description and have been shielded from the "real world," then it is understandable why you may have fallen victim.

The catch is that most women are actually *unwilling* to choose between *Mr. Right* and *Mr. Right Now*—not unable. In fact, studies show that the female gender is far more observant and perceptive compared to men.

> Overall, women are far more perceptive than men, and this has given rise to what is commonly referred to as "women's intuition." Women have an innate ability to pick up and decipher nonverbal signals, as well as having an accurate eye for small details. This is why few husbands can lie to their wives and get away with it and why, conversely, most women can pull the wool over a man's eyes without his realizing it.

Research by psychologists at Harvard University showed how women are far more alert to body language than men. They showed short films, with the sound turned off, of a man and woman communicating, and the participants were asked to decode what was happening by reading the couple's expressions. The research showed that women read the situation accurately 87 percent of the time, while the men scored only 42 percent accuracy.[8]

As that passage points out, "women's intuition" is an ability you should and must nurture. Most women instinctively know when a man is *Mr. Right Now*, or at least if he exhibits "player tendencies." On the other hand women know when they are in the presence of *Mr. Right*. Yet due to expectations by friends and family, society or raw emotion, you may stray over to the "wrong Mr." Don't let this be you.

### What are the repercussions of choosing the "wrong Mr."?

Choosing the "wrong Mr." over a period of time will inevitably leave you jaded and may eventually lead to the downfall of your love life—namely with *Mr. Right*. How so? Every time a normal person experiences something unpleasant as a result of an action, they will expectedly become more biased against achieving success through that action. If this is not fixed or rectified, then the cycle repeats itself to the point where a woman may become bitter or jaded. What man of quality (*Mr. Right*) wants to deal with an old and bitter hag?

However, if you choose *Mr. Right* when you are only seeking a *Mr. Right Now*, you may end up in an undesired relationship or worse— you may pick up a stalker.

---

[8] Pease, Barbara. Allen Pease. "Why Women Are More Perceptive: The Definitive Book of Body Language." Random House, 2006.

Now that you know the importance of picking the "right Mr.", lets find them online.


## MR. RIGHT

This is the guy that you ultimately want to end up with. Unlike men who do not have a strict biological clock, it is *imperative* that all women who wish to marry should strive to meet *Mr. Right* before their mid-thirties. This is true even if you do not desire children. It all comes down to desirability.

Although seemingly chauvinistic, women are primarily judged by their appearance, first and foremost. As explained in *The Men's Guide*, the proof is all around you. All you have to do is look to the success of the fashion industry and beauty products which earn billions of dollars per year. As women get older, gravity sets in and those perky 18 year old features begin to sag and fade. Because of that, it is essential that you get your life in order and align yourself with "wifey" characteristics, beginning no later than around ages 25-27.

### *Signs that you are "ripe" for Mr. Right*

1. You are 22 to 30 years of age and maintain your physical appearance.
2. You are established (have own place, own car, career).
3. You are no longer in your "attention whore phase".
4. You do not mind the idea of being submissive.
5. You want to get married, love the idea of being loved, and are ready to/or would like to move forward with having children.

Throughout the book, I touched on each of these items, namely in chapter one. Overall it is key to "step your game up" if you are at this phase in life. If you are in your mid to late 20's (or older) and do not have a penny to your name, no car, and have no standards in terms of the men you deal with, it is time to grow up before it's too late.

It's also important that you are over your "I just want to be seen" phase, better known as the "attention whore phase". If your profile page contains upwards of 100 photos and you are over 25 years old, it is time to work on yourself as a person if you are serious about meeting *Mr. Right*. Instead of worrying about guys commenting on your pictures, join a professional networking group, volunteer at the local "Y" or take up art classes. It's an eerie feeling seeing a 30+ year old woman attention-whoring herself and hitting on college guys. Do *not* be her! If by chance you are in your late teens or early 20's, get all of that stuff out of your system. Get to know what's out there. Hell, hit spring break in Cancun or Panama City Beach a few times and get in the wet t-shirt contests. Do what you need to do so that when it comes time to settle down, you will not need to look back or think twice.

Being ready for *Mr. Right* also means being ready to submit. This does *not* mean being his doormat or plaything. In a healthy relationship, both the man and the woman must be ready and willing to put their relationship first in order to make things work. Nowadays, there are so many women who cling to the notion of being independent and self-sufficient to the point that it seems like you are being too aggressive and masculine. Don't over do it. Lastly, you should welcome or at least be open to the idea of having a future with one special person.

Showing your "readiness" for *Mr. Right* online is simple. Post recent and attractive photos of yourself—but don't over do it. You may want to briefly mention in your introduction or "about me" section that you live alone, have a career, etc. Use proper grammar. If you browse into a man's page who fits the criteria, proceed with the lessons learned in Chapter 3. Here are some signs you are staring at the profile page of a *Mr. Right*:

## *Characteristics of Mr. Right*

1. He is college educated and/or has a career (check his "Education" and "Occupation" sections).

2. He mentions on his page that he lives alone.

3. His profile music reflects maturity (he listens to r&b, soul, soft rock or jazz).

4. He has a clean, mature look in his photos (his hair is neat, he wears nice clothes and some suits, etc).

5. He has the characteristics of the "green" men described in Chapter 2.

*Keep in mind that he still could be an experienced player. If you are seeking a *Mr. Right* and he exudes these characteristics, it does not necessarily mean he's a keeper. Keep your eye on him.

## MR. RIGHT NOW

Face it ladies. It's time to get honest. Some of you don't quite have it together yet. It's okay—a good number of men don't have it together either. If you know deep down that you are not ready to settle down with one guy, then meeting a *Mr. Right Now* online is the way to go.

We are all human so it's alright to admit that you want to be satisfied sexually and to pursue that desire. The other day, I was interviewed by an internet podcast radio show and the host and I joked about various women who throw out disclaimers after having uncommitted sex. As I explained on that show, around every 3 out of 4 women I have been with say the following after having sex with me for the first time:

"Wow, I normally don't do anything like this. I think I just got caught in the moment."

"Just so you know, that is not something I do all the time."

"I don't want you to think I'm a ho."

With that said, I am not saying that you need to put your business out there either. But if you are grown and responsible enough to handle uncommitted sex, you should be grown and responsible enough to own up to it and not feel the need to explain yourself. Just acknowledge it for what it is. Besides, most guys already know that this probably wasn't the first time you "got down" before the end of the 1st quarter. So if by chance he makes it to your end zone, it is okay to celebrate.

### Signs that you may be ready for Mr. Right Now

1. You still desire sex and/or attention from multiple people.
2. You are still bitter from past relationships.
3. You broke up with your most recent ex within the past couple of months.
4. You think all men are dogs.
5. Your life is not yet in order.

Being a woman has its own challenges. While times are rapidly changing, having uncommitted sex is still a taboo subject for women. Yet as I just explained, you must be totally honest with yourself and your needs. If your needs cannot be met with one man, do not commit. End of story.

Bitterness and anger also plays a key role. If your heart is still weak or sensitive from a past relationship or if you feel the need to lash out at anything with a penis, this is *not* the time to be in the market for *Mr. Right*. Time and time again, women believe that the best way to get over a guy is to get *under* another one. While that helps in the short-term, the only proven way to get over anyone is time, patience and self-improvement. While getting *under* another man shouldn't be an issue, keep in mind that there is a possibility of you getting attached to a fling. If you know you are a leech for love, do not put yourself in this situation. I will talk about this more in a bit.

If your life is not where it needs to be yet or if you are a bit younger, getting yourself a *Mr. Right Now* is a viable option. Some examples of your life not yet being in order include, living at home with your parents, not knowing how to cook or take care of yourself, not owning your own transportation or simply being under 21. If you are 21 years of age or under, be careful not to settle for anyone—even if he seems like he's the perfect guy. If you still feel the urge to wear skimpy clothes and dance in front of strange on lookers, then you will not be happy.

### *Characteristics of Mr. Right Now*

1. He insists on meeting quickly.
2. He makes subtle or overt sexual references.
3. He asks you various questions about your physical features, especially sexual organs (breasts, butt, and hips).
4. He has photos of himself flexing or showing off his body.
5. He doesn't have his life in order.

## <u>YOU CANNOT CHANGE HIM</u>

Women who try to change *Mr. Right Now* into *Mr. Right* are the driving force behind the reasons that women stay in relationships or long-term "friends with benefits", despite being unhappy. Deep down women find this exciting and challenging. And men know this. I have personally been guilty of having a physical relationship with a woman or two that I knew deep down wanted to be my girlfriend. But as long as everything is kept open and honest, there is generally nothing wrong with that…usually.

Once the woman makes subtle attempts to change him into *Mr. Right*, the line starts to get blurred. Men can pick up on this and many will emulate *Mr. Right* to keep her happy and maintain his steady supply of sex. A while back, a previous "friend with benefits" tried to get me to meet all of her friends and hang out with them. When I politely declined, it nearly became an obsession. "Why can't you just hang out with us?!" At the time, I thought little of it until I met someone else who I eventually started a relationship with. Once I told the "friend" about my new relationship, she was crushed. Despite being upfront with her, she allowed herself to be carried away by her hopes.

The lesson here is this: **DO NOT SETTLE**. If you know what you want, do not settle for anything less. If you go to a restaurant and order steak and they bring out a salad instead, wouldn't you say something? Of course you would. The same goes for the men you deal with. As stated back in Chapter 3, you must be realistic and deal with a player correctly. No matter how much you might like him, you cannot change make him into the man of your dreams.

On the flipside, *Mr. Right Now*-seekers must be careful not to get attached to their flings. If you are dealing with a fling and feel yourself beginning to develop feelings, recognize them for what they are and act appropriately. To spare your heart, you may have to pull back.

# Chapter Eight – Vacation Dating and Flings

# VACATION DATING

Since it is highly unlikely that you will run into *Mr. Right* while away on vacation, this chapter is primarily for the ladies who seek *Mr. Right Now*. In Chapter 8 of *The Men's Guide*, I talked about how the fellas can use social networking sites while on vacation to meet women at his destination. Beyond the obvious prize of getting "foreign booty," the goal of that chapter was to illustrate how having many options makes your trip more fun. If a guy goes on vacation and *knows* that he stands a very likely chance of meeting cute women who are looking to hook up with him, it increases his confidence. And thanks to his confidence, he will appear more attractive and will likely be more successful.

Although confidence plays a role for women, the challenge is different. It is not difficult for the average woman to get uncommitted sex from a man—in fact it is almost *too* easy. The challenge is finding a man who is attractive enough and worthy enough for your standards. Sit back ladies. I'm about to give you some serious game. Here's how you do it.

### Traveling within the United States

If you are within the United States, then Vacation Dating is easy—all you need to do is go to the "browse" or "find members" area and search within a 10 or 20 mile radius of your destination. Keep in mind that in order to allow enough time, you should start scoping out the men at your destination around two to three weeks prior to your departure. As described in Chapter 3, all you simply have to do is show interest in the guys you think are "hot".

Let's say you're visiting Miami. Beginning about two to three weeks before your adventure, start sending friend requests or invites to your guys of choice and attach a note to the request similar to the following:

"Coming to Miami.  Where are all the good clubs?"

or

"Going to Miami in 2 weeks.  Any tips for a tourist?  What should I bring? :)"

His reaction will show you exactly what kind of man he is.  If he replies quickly in a note and gives you paragraph upon paragraph of detail, he might be desperate.  Take his advice, thank him and move on.  Desperation is not sexy and is a trait most stalkers have.

If he doesn't reply, he is either not interested or was too preoccupied.  You could try again after a few days but realize that this might make *you* look desperate.  I do not recommend this— even if he replies the second time, he is more likely to treat you as an option rather than value you as a priority.

If he replies with some good advice and it isn't too wordy, gradually shift the conversation to talking about him.  If he knows how to conduct a proper conversation everything should just flow. If by chance, he hasn't proposed meeting or exchanging phone numbers after five or six exchanges, you could say something like, "You seem like a cool guy.  Maybe we can hang out when I get there."  If his response is anything less than "sure," let him go.  If he agrees, leave him your number.  However, realize that this might be the type of guy that needs to be spoon-fed suggestions, similar to a Momma's Boy.

Once you are on the phone with him, keep the call long enough to get the essentials, such as his job, what he does for a living and to get a good sense of who he is.  However, it should still be relatively brief.  After all he is out of state and is only good for *one* thing (wink wink).  Arrange an approximate date and time when he can show you around.

*Traveling outside of the United States*

Traveling outside of the United States can be tricky, mainly due to the foreign language barrier. If traveling to a non-English speaking country, I strongly advise that you learn the language of the locals. Although English is widely spoken throughout the world, it is more alluring if you can speak in the native tongue. Moreover it is safer, in the event you get lost or need help from someone who does not speak English.

Another thing that makes "vacation dating" in a foreign country more challenging is the way that social networking sites allow you to browse the locals. Unlike the United States which allows you to search by zip code, most other countries do not have this feature. What's worse is that many countries do not allow you to filter by geography at all—the only way to find out where a guy lives is by going to his page and looking for his location. This can be quite frustrating. An exception to this is Canada, which allows searching on postal codes and Brazil, which allows narrowing your prospects by region. If meeting guys out of the country is on your "to-do" list, definitely check your favorite social networking site to see if that country is "search-friendly."

*From MySpace to another place*

Now that you've found your guy or guys, it is important to manage your phone calls effectively. As explained a moment ago, calls should be kept only long enough for the essentials. If your agenda is only on the physical end, then do not start a relationship with him. Staying on the phone too long, while talking about your goals and dreams will send him mixed messages about your intentions and will hurt you two in the long run. Plus it may hurt your long distance phone plan! Check with your phone company or purchase a low cost calling card. (This is a great excuse to keep calls short if it is an international call).

Once you've had the chance to chat with him and discuss the idea of "hanging out," leave him alone until you arrive. In the event he's a womanizer or just a plain fool, it's best to have a multiple men lined up. (More tips on organizing multiple men in Chapter 9).

When you arrive at your destination, budget your time accordingly. It is best to hang out with a "foreign hottie" for the first time *before* the parties begin that evening. In addition to safety reasons, it gives you more of a reason to enjoy in the spoils of a foreign fling, including possible dinner and more activities that will be going on. Then once you go to a party with your friends later on, you won't be too bent out of shape if the party isn't all you wanted it to be.

If you follow this advice, you should have at least one guy you can look forward to spending quality time with. And when you do hook up with him (or them), thank Your Royal Flyness.

### More Travel Tips

If you can help it, travel with friends and have a way to communicate with all of them—even if you have to use a prepaid phone plan. On your keychain, belt buckle or somewhere else on you, keep a whistle, pepper spray or some other device in the event of danger. If you must go solo, at least make an effort to meet other girls from that area who you can get to know and trust— social networking sites are good for this too. There are way too many cases of women on vacation who have gone missing. Trust your gut and intuition.

## FLINGS

What if vacation dating is not your thing, but you'd still like a fling? The same rules apply to finding *Mr. Right Now:* find a hot guy, send a friend request and/or a note, and evaluate his response. However, what if you want something quicker…like…tonight?

## Craigslist

One of the quickest times I ever met a woman off the internet was through Craigslist.org. We met within minutes of first communicating through that site.

I know what you're probably thinking. "Craigslist is a site that people go to sell tickets or offer apartments for rent! Do you mean to tell me that you can find guys on Craigslist too?" My answer to you is, "Absolutely."

To effectively use Craigslist for a fling, create a personal ad and put up your best photos. (If you wish to remain anonymous, make sure the photo either blurs your face or cuts it out altogether). If you go this route, begin by creating a separate email address, as it will be easier to track who's who. Once that is done, log onto www.craigslist.org and click on your geographic preference. In the "personals" section select "women seeking men" or "casual encounters" and follow the rest of the instructions to post.

### Your ad

In speaking with various women, especially those who have used this site, most have attested to the numbers of men who claim to want a relationship but end up just wanting booty. For this reason, it's best to get right to the point without sugarcoating if all *you* want is booty. However, it can be done tastefully without seeming too "skanky." For example:

> **Subject:** 23 year old white female looking for fun tonight
>
> **Body:** I'm bored and cooped up in my apartment with no plans tonight....wanna hang out? I'm 23, 5'7, 115lbs, and cute as you can see. I'm NOT looking for a relationship and I'm open to just letting the night flow. Let's grab a bite and whatever happens, happens. Email me at least 2 full body

photos, your name and tell me about yourself. If you have myspace, leave your page link, too.

Following your ad, leave your best photos and get ready for your inbox to flood. Evaluate each message the same way you would evaluate any MySpace prospect and proceed accordingly.

*Note: I do not recommend Craigslist for browsing men, nor do I recommend looking for *Mr. Right* on this site. I have heard way too many horror stories. You are better off posting your information and filtering the guys who respond to your ad. Keep in mind that you may receive some wacky replies.

# Chapter Nine - Handling Multiple Men, Stalkers and Other Problems

B efore jumping online and jumping on a guy, it is critical that you take heed to issues such as organization, safety and other challenges you may face. Don't worry ladies— after reading this chapter, you will be well on your way to finding *Mr. Right* or *Mr. Right Now.* First, let's start with organizing your men.

## ORGANIZING MEN

If you read the *The Men's Guide*, you would already know that I dedicated an entire chapter to organizing women off the internet. Although the same challenges in remembering information about a guy exist for women, it is normally not as big of a deal. Most women tend to have better memories and are thus, less susceptible to forgetting important information. However, if by chance you are single and on the prowl, there is nothing wrong with being organized. Let me present to you...Microsoft Powerpoint!

---

## HIS NAME

- AGE
- PHONE NUMBER
- HOW YOU MET
- CITY (STATE)
- MR. RIGHT? MR. RIGHT NOW?
- HEIGHT, WEIGHT, PHYSICAL FEATURES
- INTERESTING FACTS

PHOTO(S)

---

Microsoft Powerpoint is my tool of choice to organize my prospects. It should also be yours, if you are dealing with multiple men. The following is a passage directly from Chapter 9 in *From MySpace to My Place: The Men's Guide to Snagging Women Online.* I have only changed certain words to suit the ladies:

*For each Powerpoint "slide," the title should contain the man's name. For each layout, you should always choose the split layout—allowing you to import his picture(s) on one side and his vital information on the other. For his picture(s), paste full-body shots to give you an accurate idea of exactly who you are dealing with. In the vital information side, include his age, phone number (how it was exchanged), physical features, and some interesting, unique facts about him. If you want to be thorough, include the entire message exchange in the "Notes" section below the slide. Ladies, if you do this for every man you meet, you will have no problem remembering who's who. For every city you travel to on vacation or otherwise, you should create a separate Powerpoint presentation. This makes it easier for you to organize and sort your fellas.*

Not only will you stay organized with your prospects, but you will have an easy time managing his links and photos, which can be dragged onto the Powerpoint slide or pasted directly onto the slide. And by keeping track of what he says in your notes section, you will be able to refresh your memory about what you two have discussed in the past.

## ANONYMITY

Is there *anything* on your MySpace page that would be embarrassing if your mom saw it? How about your little cousin or your boss? The answer is probably, "Yes." With that said, there are a few safeguards you should enact, ASAP!

According to an article written by About.com, there are employers who use MySpace and other social networking sites to scope out candidates for employment. It goes on to say:

According to SimplyHired (one of the top job search engines) Vice President of Marketing Phil Carpenter, "These companies look through the right lens, understand the communication skills of this generation, and are willing to set aside their biases."

You might be surprised at some of the companies that have MySpace profiles. Some of them are companies that are known for being very traditional. However, they are all cognizant of the fact that they need employees, and they are willing to think outside the typical recruiting box to attract this generation of job seekers.[9]

You must also realize that it is quite easy for friends, co-workers and stalkers alike to find you. After entering someone's name and their approximate location, just about anyone on MySpace can be found. This can be a blessing and a curse, altogether—and for obvious reasons.

My suggestion is that if you have a name that is somewhat unique, like "Orphelia Rubbenstubben" then I advise you to make your page private or at least omit your last name and only include the final initial. This would make it more difficult for someone to view your profile and pictures without your knowledge. In our example, your name would be reduced to "Orphelia R." Similarly, if you live in a small town, you may want to change your location to a larger city that is not too far away. This also makes it more difficult for people to find you. If you want "Secret Service" level security, you can require that all persons who wish to access your page provide your last name or email address. Even after this point, you would still have to approve them before they can view your profile.

On Facebook profiles, anonymity is especially a concern since so much more personal information is usually given. Facebook

---

[9] Doyle, Alison. "MySpace and Job Searching." Finding a Job On MySpace. (Year Accessed 2009). http://jobsearch.about.com/od/jobsearchblogs/a/myspacejobs.htm.

profiles normally contain information such as interests and hobbies, and each profile usually contains more photos due to "tagging" (when someone puts up a picture and "tags" you in their photo). In addition, it is not uncommon for people to put their instant messenger screen names or even phone numbers on their pages. Again, consider only including the first initial of your last name, especially if you have a unique name.

## STALKERS

A stalker is the guy who will not leave you alone. He just doesn't get it. He doesn't know what "no" means. He is obsessed. Granted, some of you ladies need to be more effective in communicating more plainly. Men are horrible at reading subliminal messages. Again, pay careful attention to the "gentle, but straightforward" approach in Chapter 4.

Let's assume that you've been straightforward with a guy and he will not leave you alone online. Hopefully this has not progressed to the telephone or to your doorstep. If you keep receiving notes from an online stalker, you can do one or more of the following:

1. Block him
2. Report him
3. Create a new account

If you pick up a stalker, perhaps one of the easiest things to do is to block him. Just about all social networking sites have the "block" button in clear view in case you need to use it. If you have exhausted trying to get him to go away, it is time to block him. This will prevent any future messages from his account going to you.

Your next option is to report him to the administrator, normally referred to as "member services," "member safety," and the like. Doing so normally requires you to enter a reason. Do not sugarcoat. Explain to them exactly what has been going on. The best part about this feature is that it's anonymous so there will not be any way for him to figure out who reported him. In most instances, this member's account will be removed within a few hours—especially if other claims are being made against him. And once a page is removed, there is very little chance it will be restored. If by chance he continues to harass you by creating a new account, you may want to consider opening a new account. This will make it very difficult to find you, since your page link would also change.

It is rare that any man can stalk you online if you've effectively performed all three of these steps. However, if a stalker remains persistent, gets your personal information or harasses you, call 9-1-1 immediately or file a police report.

### *Signs that you are looking at the profile of a stalker*

1. He shows signs of being a Lover, Momma's Boy or a Softie, as explained in Chapter 2.

2. He messages you back too quickly or sends you multiple messages before you reply.

3. He seems to worship you, even if you met online recently. Be wary of a guy who gives you too many compliments.

## STALKERS IN "FRIENDS" CLOTHING (MALE FRIENDS)

What if you give a guy the gentle, but straightforward approach and he counters with the "Let's just be friends" line?

As my friend King Flex says, "A male friend is a guy who hasn't tapped that ass yet." Ladies I *know* that many of you will not take this well. But you need to be totally honest with yourselves and realize that it is very rare that a man who approaches you would genuinely want to be your friend after being rejected. In reality, he may *settle* for friendship, hoping that one day he can get his foot in the door. This is why the, "I only see you as a friend" line doesn't work with a lot of guys. If he's a softie, he'll hang around and be the best friend he can be, praying that you will reward him some day. Of course, he'd never admit this to your face.

Many of you ladies know this and use it to your advantage. If that's what you choose to do, then fine. However, it *will* come back to "bite you in the ass" sooner or later. Let me share a story with you.

A friend of mine in my college days used to date this guy. Let's call them Janelle and John. Although Janelle did not find John especially attractive, she would always hang out with John. I found this arrangement fascinating and used to ask her why she hung out with a guy she wasn't attracted to. Yet looking beneath the surface, it was easy to see the reason.

While Janelle was a younger college student with no transportation, John had a car, a decent job and his own place. Furthermore, the area was somewhat rural so it was easy to get bored. After some prodding, Janelle admitted to me that she kept John around for the free meals, the movie dates and to keep her from getting bored on campus. However this came to an end after she grew tired of the constant phone calls from John, especially after other guys she found attractive started coming around. After admitting to John that she was not interested, it took him a while to "get the hint" and leave her alone. The lesson here: nothing is free. Rarely, if ever, will a guy give you something and not expect anything in return.

Generally, a guy can only be your friend if he does not find you attractive enough to "hit it" or if you are related to him. Other than that, be highly skeptical of any man who claims that he just wants to be your friend. If you turned around and bent over one day, don't think for one second he wouldn't take advantage of that.

Many of you may ask why I am still friends with "Janelle." Very few guys have the self-control and enough options to have platonic friendships with women, without any expectations beyond a friendship. Once a man has been through his player stage and realizes the value of his manhood, he no longer feels the need to "bang" every female in sight.

# Chapter Ten – Conclusion

I n the beginning of this book you learned how to create an effective social networking profile that will help you attract the "right Mr." Overall, less is more. Always be true to yourself. Next you learned how to effectively categorize men based on their profiles: the men to avoid (red), the ones to exercise caution with (yellow), and the ones to go for (green). Whenever possible, go for the "green" men, as this will ultimately lead to better results, regardless of seeking *Mr. Right* or *Mr. Right Now.* Later, we walked through ways to express your interest in a guy without coming off too needy and maintaining a flare of femininity. Never overdo it or he might take advantage! Next you learned how to conduct conversations properly, including how to let him down in a gentle, but straightforward manner in the event he rubs you the wrong way.

In the second half of the book, we showed you exactly what to say and what *not* to say when talking to men on the phone. Again, less is more. Do not challenge him or play unnecessary phone games. This lead right into how you should conduct yourself before, during, and after a first date. Pay careful attention to hygiene, take the proper safety precautions and have fun. Next we described in detail how to identify *Mr. Right* and *Mr. Right Now,* based on his profile page. In addition, we gave you signs on how to figure out which "Mr." you are ripe for, given your situation. Take heed. After this chapter, we discussed how to use the men you meet online to your advantage when you go on vacation or decide to have a fling. Ladies, this will surely bring some "spice" into your lives once you open yourself to the thousands of eligible men waiting for you in cyberspace. Lastly, we taught you how to organize the men you meet and how to handle any possible problems you might encounter as a result of dating someone online. It is a dangerous world out there so take that advice to heart.

This book has been your *key* to finding *Mr. Right* or *Mr. Right Now* online. All you have to do is turn it and the world is yours.

## CONCLUSION

I would like to thank each and every one of you for reading this all out, comprehensive *Ladies' Guide*. I am extremely proud of this book—not just because I wrote it, but because I know that the advice and lessons within will help many women successfully meet the men they desire, no matter which "Mr." she desires. I truly hope you enjoyed this book and that you encourage others to pick it up as well. Please be sure to leave a testimonial on my website at **www.MySpaceToMyPlace.com** and be sure to add our myspace page at **www.myspace.com/theladiesguide**. If you would like one-on-one coaching with me, please visit the website for details.

# Glossary of Online Abbreviations and Emoticons

## Chat Abbreviations

lol – laughing out loud

lmao – laughing my ass off

rotflmao – rolling on the floor, laughing my ass off

smh – shaking my head

ttyl – talk to you later

wtf – what the fuck

str8 – straight

brb – be right back

w/e – whatever

ty ; tx – thank you; thanks

yw – your welcome

j/k – just kidding


For more abbreviations, visit
http://www.sharpened.net/glossary/acronyms.php


## Emoticons

:) Smiley face; can also use :-)

;) Wink; sly, devious or even polite; can also use ;-)

:( Sad face; can also use :-(

:-\ Not satisfied; Undecided; not really "feeling it" (one of my favorites)

O:) Angel face ("I'm innocent")


For more emoticon meanings, visit
http://www.alphadictionary.com/articles/imglish/emoticons_emo
t.html

# Recommended Reads

**FROM MYSPACE TO MY PLACE: THE MEN'S GUIDE TO SNAGGING WOMEN ONLINE**
**BY YOUR ROYAL FLYNESS**

**THE ART OF GOLD DIGGING**
**BY TARIQ NASHEED**

**WHY MEN LOVE BITCHES**
**BY SHERRY ARGOV**